In *Repurposed*, Pastor Noe talks about the realities of ~~~~~ in a broken world while clinging to the promises of God. This book walks through Romans 8, maybe my favorite chapter in the Bible. As Noe shows you, purpose begins by discovering who Christ is, what He's done for you, and what He intends for you. No one is the same after reading Romans 8. You won't be the same after reading this book.

J.D. Greear, Ph.D., pastor, The Summit Church, Raleigh-Durham, North Carolina, and author of *Just Ask*

Many Christians have wondered how to experience victory in Christ when doubts, fears, sins, and guilt of the "old self" plague and assault their thought life every day. In Noe Garcia's new book *Repurposed*, he takes the reader on an unflinching journey through Romans 8 to look at how God can repurpose our failures, our pain, and our sin for His glory and our good. *Repurposed* is a discipleship resource for anyone desiring to mature as a Christian.

Robby Gallaty, pastor, Long Hollow Church and author of *Replicate* and *Recovered*

Noe Garcia is a pastor's pastor. I love his honesty and candor of his personal life that is grounded with biblically based insights. In a season where we have all questioned God's purpose, Pastor Noe helps to recenter and prepare us for the new normal. I'm excited to endorse this book, it will bless your soul!

Dhati Lewis, lead pastor, Blueprint Church

This isn't a clever book; it's a true story of our God who can turn messes into messages. Just like God repurposed Noe's story, I believe God will use this book to help bring restoration, healing, and hope to so many.

Brad Jones, Atlanta city pastor, Passion City Church

Noe's story of God's redemptive power is a great reminder of how God can take our mess and turn it into His message. This story is real, raw, and filled with God's grace.

Miles McPherson, pastor, Rock Church and former NFL player

God can speak so powerfully to others when we open our hearts and honestly share our struggles. I am grateful that my friend Noe Garcia has done that in *Repurposed*. He bares his soul and the most vulnerable places in his journey, which ultimately leads to healing and hope. If you are walking a similar path or want to minister more effectively to those who are, this is a book you will want to read and refer to often.

Kevin Ezell, president, North American Mission Board, SBC

I have seen up close the life-changing power of Christ in and through Noe Garcia. You'll find Noe's story engaging and his biblical application personally helpful. This book is the outpouring of a man who walks intimately with Christ.

Dr. Nick Floyd, senior pastor, Cross Church

Every Christian at some point has wondered, *How will God use "this" in my story . . . for His glory?* Often we see our struggles different than God sees them. In this book, Noe gives us a front row seat into God's redemptive power using Romans 8 to show us that God never wastes any experiences in our life, whether good or bad.

Marcus Hayes, lead pastor, Crossroads Baptist Church

RE
PUR
POSED

NOE GARCIA

REPURPOSED

HOW GOD TURNS YOUR MESS INTO
HIS MESSAGE

B&H
PUBLISHING
NASHVILLE, TENNESSEE

Published by B&H Publishing Group
Nashville, Tennessee

Dewey Decimal Classification: 234.3
Subject Heading: BIBLE. N.T. ROMANS 8 / GRACE
(THEOLOGY) / SALVATION

All Scripture is taken from the English Standard Version, ESV®
Text Edition: 2016. Copyright © 2001 by Crossway Bibles, a
publishing ministry of Good News Publishers.

Cover design by Jeff Miller, FaceOut Studio.
Cover background image by Reddavebatcave/shutterstock.
Author photo by AmberJoy Photography.

1 2 3 4 5 6 7 • 25 24 23 22 21

To my beautiful wife, Clancey, and my children,
Baylen, Mamie, Hallie, and Fallon.
Your lives have brought sweet healing to my soul.

Contents

Broken

Having Been Fractured or Damaged and No Longer in One Piece or in Working Order

*B*roken. That's a word we can all relate to.

It means something is damaged, not in one piece, no longer in working order.

You have probably been there. It's more than a broken heart; it's a shattered one. Brokenness shatters your hopes and dreams and leaves you in a desolate place. Your soul feels empty, and your life's purpose seems to be lost. You feel like you're at the point of no return, beyond repair.

This is how I felt for most of my life.

In high school I was seen as a highly relational, charismatic guy. I was a football and basketball star, homecoming king, and voted class favorite. Pretty cool for a high schooler, huh? But the picture painted on the outside was very different from what was going on inside. If you were to peel back the layers of my soul, you would find a broken and shattered young man. I was depressed, hopeless, and simply tired of living. I wasn't in one piece, and I certainly wasn't in working order. I was damaged and dysfunctional. I felt like my life was so broken that there was no possible way for me to be put back together. I was damaged beyond repair.

My coping mechanisms became drugs, sex, and alcohol. Did they ever really fill me? No, but they numbed me enough that I wouldn't feel the pain. But eventually, even drugs, sex, and alcohol couldn't numb what I was feeling. They were simply Band-Aids on a much deeper wound.

At the age of eighteen, I completely hit rock bottom. I was a year out of high school, not attending college, living in a duplex with two other friends, and partying every night. To be frank, I felt like a loser. I was sinking deeper and deeper and thought there was only one way out.

Suicide.

My Mess

I can remember this day as if it were yesterday. There I was, drunk and drugged. Sitting in a room filled with laughter and impaired people. Everyone seemed to be having the time of their lives, except for me. My ship was sinking, and it was time for me to jump.

I was tired of it all. I was tired of trying to fix the mess I had made of my life. A trail of abuse and broken relationships was all I knew. Hopelessness and depression were the only stable things in my life. I was done.

I went outside about midnight and looked up into the sky. The moon was bright, and the stars were so clear it was almost as if God was showing off His creation. I looked up and prayed what may sound like a silly prayer, but it was one last desperate attempt for love. I told God I wouldn't commit suicide if He showed me that He was here for me. I asked Him for a shooting star. I said, "God, if you are out there and if you are God, then would You please show me a shooting star? Then I will know that You are real. If You do this for me,

> I was tired of it all. I was tired of trying to fix the mess I had made of my life. A trail of abuse and broken relationships was all I knew. Hopelessness and depression were the only stable things in my life.

I will know that You hear me and love me, and I promise I won't commit suicide, and I'll change my life."

I was looking for hope. Something that would tell me there is a reason to live. I sat there for about thirty minutes, and anger began to boil within me because I felt like God could have quickly shown me a shooting star, but He didn't. It was almost as if He were telling me, "Do it. I don't have plans for you." It was a slap in the face and almost proved my worst fear that I was beyond repair, and He didn't want me either. Tears streamed down my face because I knew what this meant for me. If the God of the universe didn't want me, then there was no point in living. I went inside and carried out my suicide plan. Tears streamed down my face.

I went into a bedroom while the party continued, and I closed the door behind me. I will spare you the details, but a friend "happened" to notice that I was gone from the party and went looking for me. He came into the room and found me with a belt around my neck. He became hysterical and yelled out to me, running toward me and hugging me. He held me as we both shed tears of despair. I wanted to escape the pain, and this seemed like the best option at the time. At eighteen, I was ready to throw my life away because I believed a lie from the enemy that I was too far gone and too broken.

His Message

My suicide attempt was a sobering moment for me. I was at the end of my rope and realized just how broken I was. I moved in with my grandmother and slept on her couch to try to escape the life I was involved in. My days consisted of working out, playing basketball, and working double shifts as a waiter.

Every Friday night I would attend the open gym at the Salvation Army. The chaplain let us play basketball for hours as long as we stayed to listen to a short devotion. I had attended in the past, but never really listened to the gospel message. I typically ignored it and ridiculed his teachings. I thought it was for the "other" people listening. But this particular Friday night was different.

It was weeks after my suicide attempt, and my soul was fragile. I was discouraged and knew I needed to change my life. That night I heard the gospel in a way that I had never heard it before. The gospel was shared, the invitation was given, and there I was—crying in my seat and finally realizing that I was a sinner in need of a savior.

The chaplain gave the invitation, and I walked the aisle, broken and ashamed. I prayed a simple prayer: "God, I am not sure if You can hear me, but if You forgive me, I promise to do my best to follow You the rest of my life." I felt free, forgiven, and hopeful.

After that night everything changed! I put down the drugs, drinking, and immorality. I was eager to serve Jesus. I felt like I needed a fresh start and new beginning, so that's exactly what I did. I decided to attend East Texas Baptist University—a Christian university where no one would know about my past. I would be seen as "Noe the Christian," not "Noe the wild party guy."

Attending college was something I thought I would never do. My idea of a life after high school was getting a full-time job and starting a family. My mother and father dropped out of school at an early age, so I didn't have any pressure to attend college, but God had other plans for me. I can remember the day I packed up my car with the excitement of a new beginning. My desire was to leave it all behind and enter a new world where no one knew about the damaged areas of my life. I was starting a new chapter in my life, and the page was completely blank!

I was eighteen years old and a new follower of Christ when I entered my freshman year at a Christian university. I was filled with butterflies in my stomach and anxiety from the unknowns of a new life. In the hours leading up to orientation, I sifted through outfits looking for the one that made me feel like I could belong. I didn't have many nice clothes, but I had a few tricks that my grandmother taught me to make older clothes look new with a can of starch and an iron.

Orientation started, and I walked in feeling fresh and clean. My pants were starched with a nice crease, and my hair was perfectly faded. I had a bit of a holy swag going on. I took a deep breath, and I walked into a room filled with hundreds of students. I was instantly filled with insecurity. My holy swag imploded. I wasn't going to fit here.

The students were clean-cut, nicely dressed, and looked like they had it all together. I'm not sure what the perfect Christian college student was supposed to look like, but they seemed to fit the mold. They came from Christian homes, they knew the Bible, many of their fathers were pastors, and their future seemed bright. It wasn't their fault, but seeing them all there terrified me.

I was a Hispanic kid from inner-city Houston who came from a fatherless home. I had enough baggage for the entire university; my list of sins was deep and wide. I had piercings and tattoos, wore baggy clothes, listened to rap music, didn't know how to read my Bible, and spoke with slang. You get the picture? I stood out like a sore thumb.

If the university were a store and the students were luxury products, you could find me in the "damaged goods" section. I didn't think I would be able to make it in this new world. I was way out of my league, and I felt like it was only a matter of time before I'd quit. But I didn't give up that easily. I pressed in and got ready for what I knew would be a challenging journey.

Being on the basketball team and running cross-country helped me build instant community with like-minded guys who accepted and understood me. I felt safe in this circle, but it was impossible to hide in that small community forever. I eventually would have to interact with the other students who intimidated me. Hoops and hanging were things I could master, but talking about theology and ministry was foreign to me. I tried to engage in this community, but over time my insecurity coupled with the passive-aggressive comments began to take a toll on me. Comments about the way I looked and dressed continually reminded me that I was different. Late-night Bible studies and discussions about purity reminded me that I was damaged and too far gone. I certainly felt inferior to my peers and thought that the battle to be equal was one I couldn't win, so I accepted the position of inferiority. Jokes were thrown my way about my culture and the slang I used, so I bought into the role of the "hood guy." In fact, I began to make fun of myself just to ease the pain and accept the social position I was placed in.

My efforts to become somebody and make a better life for myself often seemed impossible. My peers were in a different league intellectually, emotionally, financially, and socially. No matter what I did or accomplished, I was still the inner-city Hispanic kid from Houston. There were times when I would drive in my car alone for miles complaining to God and asking Him why He allowed me to be born and experience the things I experienced. There were many days when I wished I were someone else. But unfortunately, at the end of my complaining session, I was still me, an inner-city Hispanic kid from Houston with a messed-up past. I was stained with an image I couldn't escape. Questions—When will I fit in and not be judged? and When will I gain the confidence to know that I am enough?—constantly ran through my mind. I wanted to be loved and accepted fully for who I was. I wanted someone to see past the rough image and realize that deep inside there was a boy yearning for love and acceptance. Instead I felt like I was met with harsh judgment and ridicule. My environment constantly reminded me that I was damaged and, even worse, made me feel like I wasn't useful.

In my exhaustion, my insecurity turned into to self-deprivation and resentment toward those around me who seemed to have it easy. The Christian student leaders were the ones who hurt me the most, and my hurt turned into anger and bitterness toward the church and other Christians.

My expectations of a Christian university were filled with acceptance, love, joy, and peace. But unfortunately, I didn't realize that Christians are still sinful individuals who possess the ability to cause great pain. For some reason, it seems like Christian wounds cut the deepest. Maybe it's because of the expectation we have for one another or because there is a sense of betrayal when it's from you own Christian family. Either way, it cuts deep.

My anger turned into action when I walked into the cafeteria and overheard one of the Baptist Students campus leaders telling the entire table that he couldn't stand me. I was thrown off guard. Couldn't stand me? What did I do wrong?

I looked in his direction, nodded, and laughed it off. After dinner I went to my dorm room and cried. I was fed up. I was sick and tired of not fitting in. I had no control of the culture I was raised in or who I was. I hated the school, I hated Christians, and I hated that I even tried to turn my life around. I settled for the fact that I was a failure and was always going to be a failure. No matter how far I ran or how many times I attempted to hit the reset button, my past didn't disappear. I would always be the inner-city Hispanic kid from Houston with the messed-up past.

So I gave up. I had entered a world I knew nothing about. One that was filled with success and achievement and one I could not obtain. I was ready to leave it.

That night I packed up my Jeep Cherokee and was ready to head back to Houston. I settled for the fact that I was damaged and could never be used. The truth is, I didn't want to go. I wanted to stay, graduate, and make something out of my life. But that seemed like a dream that would never be fulfilled.

As I began to drive off, two of my basketball team-mates came outside to say their good-byes. They shared with sincerity how God had used me to impact their lives. Their heartfelt words about the impact I made opened up my eyes. I was shocked! God was using me, and I didn't even know it. In that moment God showed me that not only *could* I be used but that He *was already* using me. It just wasn't going to look like I thought it would.

He was using my past to reach people who could relate to me. Maybe it wasn't going to be the crowd I thought it was going to be, but it would be the crowd God wanted it to be.

For the first time in my Christian life, I saw how God was using me, and it would forever change me. Right before my eyes He was repurposing all the damaged areas of my life and using them for His glory. From that point on, my life mission would be to focus on the broken and hurting. The words of Jesus would begin to echo in my heart: "It's not the healthy that need a doctor but the sick" (see Luke 5:31).

> For the first time in my Christian life, I saw how God was using me, and it would forever change me. Right before my eyes He was repurposing all the damaged areas of my life and using them for His glory.

This is not saying that Christians who "have it together" don't matter but instead that God was making clear what my mission would be. I was going to devote myself to reaching the "sick." I unpacked my car and went back into my dorm room. I felt like chains were broken and the burden was lifted.

For the next four years I shared the gospel like a mad man. I was involved in different ministries, youth groups, and anything else that came my way. I wanted everyone to hear about Christ and His redemptive work. I was a living and walking testimony of His goodness and wanted everyone to know about Him! I became a man on a mission.

The Bible is filled with characters who believed they weren't anything more than damaged goods. Their shortcomings caused them to deem themselves useless. They thought their sin was too great and their God too small.

Moses was a murderer who had a stuttering problem. He was filled with insecurity and shame and gave God a list of reasons he couldn't be used by God, but God chose him anyway.

Noah seemed to be a man who had an addiction. He couldn't put down the bottle, not to mention his dysfunctional family. Yet God considered his faith and counted it to him as righteousness.

David had a good start as a faithful shepherd boy and a horrible ending as an adulterer, yet God used him and called him "a man after God's heart."

Jeremiah argued that he was too young and couldn't speak and was terrified of the people, yet God chose him.

Last but not least, Paul. A man who hunted down and killed Christians. He alone was responsible for countless murders, and God chose him to write most of the New Testament.

Does this give you a little taste of what God can do? I don't want to diminish the consequences of sin because they are real, but I also don't want to shortchange our big and glorious God. He too is real.

I have found myself leaving God on the pages of Scripture and not allowing Him to enter my everyday life. It is hard for me to believe God wants to repurpose my life for my good and His glory, but He does. He not only wants to do it with my life, but He wants to do it with yours too.

> My prayer is that you are able to invite God into your brokenness and watch Him do what only He can through your life.

Where We're Headed

My desire is to take you on a journey through real and raw stories of brokenness while allowing Scripture to define reality and inspire hope in the deepest parts of your soul. We will do this by walking through Romans 8, a chapter of Scripture many scholars consider the greatest chapter ever written. Through this journey you will be able to see how Scripture has the power to repair, restore, and repurpose what the enemy intended for harm. My prayer is that you are able to invite God into your brokenness and watch Him do what only He can through your life.

God can take our mess and turn it into His message.

CHAPTER 1

Shame

The Painful Feeling Arising from the Consciousness of Something Dishonorable, Improper, and Ridiculous Done by Oneself or Another

Shame. That's a word we're all too familiar with.

In fact, as I write this chapter, I have to admit that I still struggle with shame. Shame from things that were done to me at an early age, shame from my sins of the past and present, shame from the things I didn't do that I know I should have done. Shame is a powerful emotion. It has the power to strip us of all hope and make us believe that our sins are too great to be forgiven. It leaves us in great despair, wondering if God can ever use us again. It causes us to walk into a room and assume that everyone is talking about us. Shame causes us to be disgusted with ourselves, tempting us to forfeit our future.

I know this feeling all too well. I wish my slate were clean and I had no sin to regret, but that's not the case for me.

For most of my life, I have found myself looking for solutions to cover the inner pain I was experiencing. Unfortunately, in my attempt to self-medicate, I made things worse and fed the monster I now call shame. Over time the monster grew bigger and stronger, and it became untamable. This monster controlled my emotions, thoughts, and behaviors. Its power seemed to be unmatched, and I soon found myself surrendering to its call. Shame became like a best friend who shows up unexpectedly and never leaves. We became inseparable. This monster still wakes me up in the middle of the night to taunt me and shows up from time to time to remind me that it will never leave me or forsake me. It's exhausting.

I'm not talking about the kind of a shame that makes you feel bad when you overeat or when you've binged on social media for hours. I am talking about the type of shame that paralyzes you. The kind of a shame that reminds you over and over that you failed. Shame that has you running when no one is chasing.

It's related to a broken relationship. A divorce. A bad habit. A failed career or a sinful decision.

Shame has no mercy or grace for its victims. It finds the weak and wounded and attaches itself to us like a bloodsucking leech. It attaches itself to the barren woman who longs to have children, to the parent with a wayward child, to the person with the pornography addiction, and to the one with a painful past. Shame has no concern for the destruction it leaves behind.

Most of us have befriended shame at one time or another. If shame is your best friend, just an acquaintance, or like a distant father who shows up from time to time, the effect is the same: debilitating. We are all too familiar with the guilt and isolation it produces. Shame ties us to the past, keeps us stuck in the present, and blinds us to the future.

> Shame has no mercy or grace for its victims. It finds the weak and wounded and attaches itself to us like a bloodsucking leech.

My Mess: Shame, Shame, Go Away

College is filled with temptation for any Christian. Supervision is rare and freedom is often abused. I started college off strong—playing basketball, running cross-country, making the dean's list, and working at the Boys and Girls Club. While I had lots of ups and downs trying to fit into the culture, I stayed on the straight and narrow. And once I saw how God was using me to bless others, things seemed to be good. Maybe too good.

In fact, things were going so well, I lost respect for the power of sin. Sin for me was a thing of the past that was dead, buried, and no longer had any power in my life. But that mentality proved to be my first mistake. Old sins began to knock on the door of my flesh, and because I had absolutely no boundaries in my life that protected me from my old sin, I slowly fell back into those sinful habits.

I ended up falling into my first "big" sin since becoming a Christian so I had no clue how to handle it. I thought something was wrong with me. How dare I fall back into the very sin Christ saved me from. Maybe I wasn't saved! Should I confess? But what If I got kicked out of school?

Predictably, shame reintroduced itself into my life. But how? I thought I was free from that as a Christian. I wanted the feeling of shame to leave my life and never come back again. I wanted it to go away! Unfortunately, shame was part of the consequence of my sin. It was there to accuse me and remind me of my shortcomings.

I didn't confess my sin right away because I was too ashamed of myself. I was afraid of the ridicule and judgment I would receive if I were open and honest with other Christians. I already had a tough time fitting in, and this would definitely prove I didn't belong there.

But there was another reason I didn't feel comfortable confessing.

> Shame was part of the consequence of my sin. It was there to accuse me and remind me of my shortcomings.

I sat quietly and listened in student-led Bible studies and watched how we started with the Word but then slowly turned to criticizing our brothers' and sisters' failures. Instead of practicing the grace we were reading about, we would shame those who were struggling. Church culture trained and conditioned us only to share the socially acceptable struggles, the ones that we are comfortable with. Even then, we would share as if they were past sins and not present. Because if they were present sins, then maybe we wouldn't be looked at as godly. I am sure I am not innocent in this, but I remember that it caused me to think I would never share any of my struggles or failures with people.

I quickly felt like there was no such thing as a "safe place." So, instead of confessing my sin, I found myself burying it even further down. Shame was telling me to hide at all cost, so I did. I lived in misery and felt so alone with my sin. I was drowning.

I felt like I was a fraud whose clock was ticking, and it was only a matter of time before I was found out. My greatest fear about my failures was not God's punishment (although I did fear it); it was the punishment from my Christian family. I knew that as far as the east is to the west God has removed my sin. But I wasn't confident that was true for Christians.

I was tired of running. I couldn't take it anymore. I was tired of the sleepless nights and the shame that was covering me. I felt like God's hand was heavy upon me, so I mustered up all the courage I had, stopped concealing my sin, and confessed to those I trusted. I remember I was terrified. I was terrified of what people would think about me. I was terrified of the potential backlash and result of my confession. The fear of being looked at or treated as less than others haunted me.

Well, I wasn't completely wrong. Some "friends" told me that they couldn't understand how a Christian could fall back into sin if he were really saved. Others distanced themselves from me so they wouldn't be seen with the "sinner."

But some embraced me, prayed with me, and helped me place healthy boundaries in place to protect me from falling again. As I matured in my walk, I realized that the Christian life is a continual life of repentance. Sin is strong and powerful and will not cease to be a part of our life on earth. Part of the consequence of sin is shame—that's exactly what sin produces. But let me encourage you: you are not alone in your struggle. Other believers out there will love you, encourage you, fight for you, and fight with you. No matter how big you think your sin is is, you are not alone!

Naked and Not Ashamed

There was a time long ago when shame didn't exist and everything was perfect—no guilt or embarrassment. But then sin entered the world and brought shame along with it.

Genesis 2:25 says, "And the man and his wife were both naked and were not ashamed." What's the point here? The Bible is communicating that even in their most vulnerable state—being naked—Adam and Eve felt no shame. They had nothing to hide from God or each other, no reason to be covered up. They walked with God and each other with utter confidence and no fear about being found out. They were pure, transparent, and naked.

The word *naked* means more than just nudity. It means they were totally open and exposed before God and man. They had no sin and nothing to be ashamed of.[1] Nothing mentally, physically, or emotionally. There was pure intimacy.

But it didn't last long. By Genesis 3 we see this bond of intimacy destroyed because of sin. Adam and Eve disobeyed God, bringing sin into the world. That sin shattered the intimacy Adam and Eve had with each other but, most importantly, with God. In Genesis 2, we saw that they were without shame and had nothing to hide. In chapter 3 they were now ashamed, hiding from God, and covering up: "And they heard the sound of the LORD God walking in the garden in the cool of the day, and the man and his wife *hid* themselves from the presence of the LORD God among the trees of the garden" (Gen. 3:8).

Ashamed and afraid, they hid from God. But there is something we can't miss in this one verse. Although their sin caused them to feel shame and want to hide, God didn't hide from them. In fact, in this text His personal name is used: *LORD God*. This is God's personal name that shows His intimate relationship with His people. Yes, their relationship would soon be distorted because of the sin that entered, but God didn't run and hide from them. What Adam and Eve experienced is what humanity will experience until Christ comes back. Any time sin enters the picture of our lives, shame is a close cousin who comes along with it. It reminds us that we failed and we should hide and cover ourselves like Adam and Eve did. It's a natural response to our sin. Welcome to the lifelong battle. But there is hope.

Paul gives us this hope in Romans 7, showing us that we are not alone in our battle with sin.

> For I do not understand my own actions. For I do not do what I want, but I do the very thing I hate. Now if I do what I do not want, I agree with the law, that it is good. So now it is no longer I who do it, but sin that dwells within me. For I know that nothing good dwells in me, that is, in my flesh. For I have the desire to do what is right, but not the ability to carry it out. For I do not do the good I want, but the evil I do not want is what I keep on doing. Now if I do what I do not want, it is no

longer I who do it, but sin that dwells within me.

So I find it to be a law that when I want to do right, evil lies close at hand. For I delight in the law of God, in my inner being, but I see in my members another law waging war against the law of my mind and making me captive to the law of sin that dwells in my members. Wretched man that I am! Who will deliver me from this body of death? (vv. 15–24)

What a passage! It's unusually comforting. It can be discouraging to know that we will have this constant battle in our lives, but on the other hand, praise God that this is normal and we are not an anomaly.

You are not some sort of freak or failure as a Christian because you still battle sin. We all fight a war within us. Some will struggle with sexual immorality and impurity. For others it may be envy, jealousy, arrogance, pride, or idolatry. It might be gossip or people-pleasing or an obsession with the opinion of others. No matter what it is, we will all have a battle. And Satan's goal is to condemn and shame us when we fail.

Another name for Satan is Accuser, and that's exactly what he does: he accuses the children of God. He attempts to condemn us and make us think we're worthless. He reminds us of our past and present sins, hoping to leave us paralyzed and drowning in our shame. The enemy is an accuser and a condemner, but we don't have to submit to his power. Shame doesn't have to win, and you don't have to hide. You can have victory!

Breaking Shame's Power

There is a part Christ plays and a part you play in breaking shame's power. Get a shovel, and let's start digging. We'll dig deep and search in your soul for the things you have been covering and hiding. The things you have done that no one knows about. We are going to bring them all out to the light. You have to be willing to face it in order to defeat it. The enemy wins his battle in the dark, and we win ours in the light.

Let me encourage you as we begin. That thing that came to mind as you were reading . . . the thing that terrifies you . . . the thing that makes you sick to your stomach when you think about it. No matter what it is, that thing doesn't stand a chance against what was done on the cross. It lost its power when Christ died and rose again. It has been defeated. That thing doesn't stand a chance! Forgiveness and grace await you on the other side of confession.

> The enemy wins his battle in the dark, and we win ours in the light.

I know you're probably tired of carrying this, but rest is on the other side of confession. And that's the first step: confession.

Acknowledgment Releases Shame

You need to do this! Acknowledging your sin will help you live freely in the present and offer hope for the future. The past is something the enemy will use consistently and aggressively to keep you spiritually paralyzed. He knows that if he can keep you living in shame, then you won't move into a life of freedom. He will remind you of the things you did wrong or the wrong things that were done to you. He wants you to feel like you are not worthy. He wants you to think that forgiveness is impossible for you. He blinds us to the future by muddying the waters of the present with phrases like, "You can't be restored," "You can't be used," "Look at how horrible you are," and the list goes on and on. If we listen to those phrases for too long, then we will begin to believe them, and our beliefs will affect our behavior.

Let's take a look at the life of David. He was a man after God's own heart, yet he knew shame very well. Shame was a close friend for most of his life. He was shamed when he was a shepherd. He was shamed in his home by his brothers. He was shamed by others when he fell and sinned. He knew shame.

David knew what it meant to sin and attempt to cover it up. It began when he saw a beautiful woman (Bathsheba) and took her for the night. She was another man's wife, but he misused his authority to take advantage of her, committed adultery, and impregnated her.

I am sure he was feeling guilt, remorse, conviction, and shame. Can you imagine? He was weak and tempted, and after accomplishing so much in his life, a moment of weakness caused it all to come crumbling down. The pursuit of pleasure led to the mistake of a lifetime. He was left with the broken pieces caused by his sin.

A one-night stand now turned into a lifetime of turmoil. Would he no longer be king if people found out? If he remained king, would people disrespect him? Would he lose the image he carefully protected?

So, what does he do? Instead of confessing his sin and repenting, he comes up with a plan. A horrible plan. Sin and shame go hand in hand, and so do dumb and dumber. That is what sin does. It makes us irrational! David wasn't logical. He wasn't thinking straight. His decision-making skills were now distorted. So he went to extreme measures. He took Bathsheba's husband and had him killed, hoping the deep dark secret would never get out. So now, not only was he drowning in his shame for his sexual sin, but he also added a murder plot to his conscience. He did not know it yet, but it was only a matter of time before everything would come crashing down.

David was deceived by thinking if he could hide his sin long enough, it would just go away. This is precisely what sin does. It makes you irrational and misleads you into thinking it's no big deal. It makes you think you can just bury it, and it will never surface. It overpromises and underdelivers. Sin entices us to do the wrong thing and then shames us when we do. Sin is strong. It's powerful. It never stays quiet. It will always find you out. Sin will cause you to plant seeds in private and will produce fruit in public.

Not to mention another little detail we must not forget—*you cannot hide your sin from God, no matter how hard you try.*

For shame to lose its power, you must acknowledge the very things that are producing it. If shame is the fruit of my sin, then I have to get to the root, so it stops producing fruit. This is incredibly hard but necessary to move forward. I may not like it, but I must acknowledge the past and accept that it happened.

Here is where you will have to be honest with yourself about what is making you feel so shameful. Is it a broken relationship? Is it something that was done to you? The poor decision you made? Whatever it may be, you must acknowledge the fact that it happened.

In Psalm 32, this is precisely what David does when he finally begins his path to freedom. For David, it took a confrontation from one of his subordinates to finally wake him up to the full effects of what he had done (2 Sam. 12). But once God used the words of Nathan to wake him up, he got to work. He starts by getting to the root issue: his sin. He uses three different terms to define what he did wrong—*transgression*, *corruption*, and *iniquity*.

All these words show that he knew what he was doing was wrong, but he did it anyway. I love that he takes ownership of his junk. He didn't point the finger at others for his failures. Instead he owned it! David committed adultery and then murder to cover it up. This led to emotional, physical, and spiritual starvation. He became weak and feeble in every area of his life because he was exhausted from hiding. As he looked back at his sin, he acknowledged that the misery he was experiencing was connected to the sin he was covering. He finally gave up and uncovered it.

Have you ever been so deep in sin, and so terrified about the consequences that came with it, that you found yourself trying to hide and cover it? Even committing new sins to cover up the old ones? If so, then you know exactly what David was talking about. If you are there now, you are probably exhausted from living a life in hiding. David shares how you can get out of hiding and live in freedom. In Psalm 32:5, he says, "I *acknowledged* my sin to you, and I did not cover my iniquity; I said, 'I will confess my transgressions to the LORD,' and you forgave the iniquity of my sin" (emphasis added).

There it is! The first step to freedom is *acknowledgment*. He acknowledged his sin! He admitted his wrongdoing that was producing shame. But he didn't stop there. Acknowledgment was only the first step.

Confession Releases Shame

David's next step was confession. You can acknowledge something without confessing it. This is where we get into habitual sin. We can admit it but not uproot it. I can walk by and stare at the weeds in my yard and acknowledge they are there, but they will continue to grow until I do something about them.

Confessing is doing something about our sin so shame doesn't continue to grow. The word *confess* means to agree with God that we missed the mark. We have sinned and fallen short. The enemy loves to fight in the dark; that is his battleground. We must bring our deepest secrets into the light. That's God's battleground, and that's where the enemy loses his power. Confessing brings our sin out of the darkness and into the light where we're able to win our spiritual fights. The dark is the enemy's territory; he loses his power in the light.

Acknowledgment and confession are where the accuser begins to lose the battle, because as we move forward to bring things out to the light, he begins to lose his grip. The worst thing to do is to conceal the things that are causing shame. If we cover our sin, then all we are doing is pouring soil on the root, which will eventually grow through.

> Confessing is doing something about our sin so shame doesn't continue to grow.

You can't just trim a weed or pour dirt over it and expect it not to grow; you have to pull it out by its root. Confession is the uprooting of the weed. When confession happens, the source of shame loses its power.

David continues in Psalm 32 and gives us a great picture of what happens when we don't confess: "For when I kept silent, my bones wasted away through my groaning all day long" (v. 3). He knew how it felt to be guilty. He knew how it felt to fall short. He was speaking about something that happened in the past, so he spoke from experience about what it's like to sin and then try to cover it up. Was he ashamed, and that's what led to his cover-up efforts? I am sure he was!

He goes on to say that God's hand was heavy upon him day and night. Think about what he was saying. All day long he felt the weight of covering his sin. He was depleted emotionally, physically, and spiritually. He says that his strength was dried up like in the heat of summer.

When I was a child, I loved watching professional wrestling. Guys like "The Ultimate Warrior" and "Super Fly Jimmy Snuka" were my heroes. They would fly from the top of the ropes and pin their opponents into a position they couldn't escape. My favorite part was to see the opponents stuck in a position they couldn't get out of. They would squirm, fight, and try every maneuver they knew, but it was obvious they were pinned and not getting out. They would realize they were stuck and tap the mat signifying that they gave up.

This is what David did. He realized his sin had him pinned and the only way he was going to get free of the sin was to tap out. He was telling us that God's hand was heavy on him, had him pinned, and he wanted relief.

I love what Charles Spurgeon says: "God's hand is beneficial when it uplifts, but it is awful when it presses down: better a world on the shoulder, like Atlas, than God's hand on the heart, like David."[2]

When we hide and conceal, not only does it produce unwanted shame, but even worse, it causes God to press down on our hearts. This leads us into misery until we come clean. The enemy will tell you it is best to cover and hide your sin for many reasons—maybe it will just go away; maybe if enough time goes by, then you will forget about it. Well, you and I both know it doesn't work that way. Satan wants to prolong your misery and the distant feeling between you and God. As long as you let him do that, God's hand will be heavy on you.

But something important needs to be said here. *It is good that God's hand is heavy on us while we are living in unconfessed sin.* Because you are His child, God's grace will not allow you to stay in hiding. The heaviness and drained feeling David felt indeed was God's grace leading him to repentance and confession so that he could finally live in freedom. God's not out to get you in trouble; the pressure you feel from His hand is like the loving discipline of a Father correcting his child, so that the child can thrive and live a fruitful life! Think about that. God will not let you sin in peace.

I always pray for my children that if there is ever any hidden sin in their lives, they will not be able to sleep or eat until they confess it. I pray that if they are in sin, they will be so miserable that their misery leads to their freedom. Our sorrow is God's grace leading us back to Him. Sin cannot be covered until it's uncovered. And that's exactly what David does here. He reveals his sin by confessing and allows the grace of God to cover it.

> God will not let
> you sin in peace.

Confession releases shame, and forgiveness covers it. Confession lifts the hand of God. This is precisely what happened to David. He confessed, and God's hand was raised.

Confession Brings Freedom

It's incredible how much freedom comes with confession. David confesses his sin, then says, "And you forgave the iniquity of my sin" (Ps. 32:5). What a powerful statement. An adulterer and a murder asked for forgiveness, and he received it. Just like that!

This word *forgiveness* means that your sin is completely cancelled. God is not going to hold it against you or hang it over your head. If I can be honest with you, others might. People will see you and identify you with your sin. You may lose some friends and be judged by others. But who cares! They don't have the power to choose your future. They don't have the power to determine how God will use you, nor does God need their permission. God doesn't need the approval of man concerning with whom, when, and where He accomplishes His purposes. It's His decision. So lift your head up high and don't live in shame.

If the Creator of the universe says you are forgiven, then the opinions of other people are simply that—their opinions. And those opinions don't hold up in God's court.

David acknowledged his sin, confessed it, and received forgiveness, and the same can happen for you. But you must take these steps. Once sin is brought into the light, no matter what it is, you no longer feel like you have to hide or try to cover it. You no longer feel like a fraud who's afraid of being found out. But instead you can walk in complete freedom now that the Creator of the universe has forgiven you. You no longer have to hang your head in shame and avoid eye contact. Now you can look people straight in the eyes, knowing they can't accuse you of anything God has pardoned you from.

David goes from talking about the misery he felt from hiding his sin in verses 3 and 4 to celebrating the freedom he now has in verse 7. Can you imagine how he must have felt covering his sin because of the shame that it brought and would continue to carry? He hid at all costs, then confessed and found freedom. He was so free that it seemed as if he didn't care what others had to say about him. He goes from hiding *from* God to hiding *in* God.

So, in other words, he is saying, *For all of you who want to judge, ridicule, and shame me, if you are wondering where I am, I am hiding in God. If you're going to get to me, you have to go through Him to find me. If you want me, you will have to go through my Father!*

What a moment! What confidence! What if we lived that way? Often we cover our stuff because we are so afraid of what people will think about us. We are so fearful of the shame it's going to produce that we hide it and shame ourselves. Imagine what our lives would look like if we stopped being enslaved to man's opinions and started walking in the freedom of Christ.

As rapper Lecrae often says, "If you live for people's acceptance, you will die from their rejection." You don't have to live this way! David pleads with you not to. Hide in Christ before it's too late!

His Message: No Condemnation

It's easier said than done, isn't it? We love to carry the burden of the things God has released us from. We don't often know how to live in freedom, and being enslaved to shame sometimes seems easier than walking in forgiveness.

We can see this in the story of the Israelites in Exodus. God performed a series of unbelievable miracles, culminating in the literal parting of a sea, to free His people from slavery and oppression at the hands of the world's greatest superpower. Until the cross, it was the greatest act of salvation in history. But as soon as they got out of slavery, the people started grumbling. First, they got thirsty and complained to Moses. Then, they got hungry. Look at what they said: "The people of Israel said to them [Moses and Aaron], 'Would that we had died by the hand of the LORD in Egypt, when we sat by the meat pots and ate bread to the full, for you have brought us out into this wilderness to kill this whole assembly with hunger'" (Exod. 16:3).

Are you kidding me? God just parted the Red Sea and drowned the strongest army in the world, and they thought He couldn't give them some lunch? But it proves the point, doesn't it? *Sometimes staying in slavery feels easier than walking in freedom.*

This is why believing God's Word is true is vital to defeating the enemy's allegations. The only way you can defeat lies is with the truth. Many Christians know about forgiveness but have a problem truly accepting it.

Do you believe He will remember your sins no more as promised in Hebrews?

Do you believe that as far as the east is from the west He will remember your sins no more, as stated in Psalm 103?

Do you believe that while you were still a sinner Christ died for you, as Paul says in Romans 5?

These are powerful truths you need to defeat the lies. Imagine if you walked in these truths and if you allowed these passages to affect your behavior. You would live as a victor and not a victim. But this is a great mystery. Why do Christians believe the whispers of a lie more than we do the roars of the truth? We don't accept the forgiveness we have been given. We would rather wallow in shame and guilt because we think, in the depth of our souls, that's what we deserve.

Romans 8 is about emancipation. In it we are told that God frees us to be His sons and daughters. We are no longer condemned by sin but redeemed through Christ. We experience emancipation. We also see the whole creation will be set free, and this freedom is eternal. God's love for us is unshakable. When we are set free by God, we are loved with an unchangeable love that keeps us free no matter what struggle we face.

But it's not as easy as it sounds. Despite God's love, we often feel trapped. We are burdened by worry, the weight of our sins, doubt, our circumstances, and more. When we cling to the burden, we lose sight of the freedom God gives us through Christ. We believe what shame says about us more than what God has to say about us. It's a cycle that's hard to defeat.

> When we are set free by God, we are loved with an unchangeable love that keeps us free no matter what struggle we face.

The great news is that in our weakness and failure to believe that He has forgiven us and washed us from our shame, the truth still remains. We are washed new because of Christ. Our lack of belief in being forgiven doesn't make us any less forgiven. It may make us bound to disbelief, but not to unforgiveness. God already took care of that.

In Romans 8:1, Paul gives us one of the most liberating verses in the New Testament: "There is therefore now no condemnation for those who are in Christ Jesus." Right out of the gate, he gives extraordinary comfort to the ordinary sinner. Let's take a deeper look.

We know what the word *now* means, don't we? It communicates immediacy. The present tense. In this very moment. If the reader is wondering when this truth will be applied, Paul is letting them know. It's applied now!

He is not saying nothing in man is condemnable, for we know that all have sinned and fallen short of the glory of God. Sin is no doubt dangerous in the life of the believer and has horrific consequences. The Christian is not safe from the effects of sin here on earth. But Paul is saying, because you are in Christ, you will not face eternal condemnation as you once would. So now that you are in Christ, you have had a course correction. He says in this moment, during the act or even after the act of sinning, right now, you are not condemned.

The word *condemnation* is a legal term. *Not condemned* means to be found not guilty of an accusation and released of all charges. This is the position of *every* believer. We stand not guilty before the judge of heavens, God! We know we are guilty of the things we have done, thought, or said, and that brings waves of shame along with it. To some degree, we feel like we deserve it, and, well, we do. But let's put this into perspective. It's like you are standing before the judge because you broke the law, and you're guilty, and before the judge bangs the gavel and condemns you, someone stands up and says, "Whatever they did, I will do their time. I will serve their life sentence. I don't care what it is. I don't care if it is murder, adultery, or theft. Whatever it is, I will take their sentence for them." This is precisely what Christ did so that we can be forgiven and set free!

We are on trial and were going to be sentenced to death because of our sin, but Christ intervened and paid the penalty. This means our past, present, and future sins could *never* condemn us. No one can bring any charges against us that will hold up in a courtroom before God. Did you read that? Maybe go ahead and read it again.

Your past, present, and future sins cannot condemn you. While they have earthly consequences, the eternal reward remains the same. Jesus already took the punishment in Himself on the cross. Every single sin has been paid for!

Christians will unfortunately continue to sin. We may feel the effects of the sin here on earth, but our standing before God does not change. Jesus does not need to attend another court date to rid you of all condemnation. The cross paid for it once and for all. Your sin from that point on can no longer condemn you and tell you that you are guilty and have a death sentence awaiting you. When the accuser points the finger at you and says, "That one is a sinner; she belongs to me," Jesus responds, "No, that one's sin has been paid for; she belongs to me." And God the Father always rules on the side of His Son.

Many Christians have been set free but live as if they were still accused and condemned. They have been released by Christ but have placed themselves in mental handcuffs and simply do not know how to defeat the shame that's attached to their sin. If you are a person who is shame and guilt ridden, let me encourage you. Let it go! Leave the cuffs in the courtroom. You are no longer tied to your crime, and you do not have to pay the time. No condemnation means no more carrying the punishment and consequences that breed shame!

He Covers Your Shame

You have no reason to be ashamed. Christ has covered all your sin for you! Once Adam and Eve sinned, shame entered the scene. Their eyes were open, and they sewed fig leaves together and made coverings to cover their shame (Gen. 3:7). But this was man's attempt at covering, and it wouldn't be sufficient. In fact, man's attempt never is.

In Genesis 3:21, you see God graciously provide for humanity's need in a way Adam and Eve couldn't do. God clothes them not with fig leaves but with animal skins. This was the first animal sacrifice that would be the anticipation of the Old Testament sacrificial system. This was a gospel foreshadow of what was to come—sin being covered by the perfect sacrificial Lamb, Jesus. Christian, what a picture for us. We are covered not by our attempts but by God's grace!

So, to the one who can relate to the wrestle between flesh and Spirit and cannot seem to get it right, and to the one who is addicted to sin, and to the one beating himself of because of the same failures over and over again, there is excellent news for you! Your sin is not your identity; the work of Christ is! We should take a praise break right here and give Him a thank-you and a hallelujah. This is a selah moment. It seems too good to be true!

A shame-free life is hard to grasp, isn't it? That is because we live in a world that continually wants to shame us. We shame one another in church. We shame one another on social media. We shame one another in sports. We shame one another in school. We love to capitalize on one another's failures. And so it's hard to grasp the truth while the world is shaming you and while you are shaming yourself.

You Can Do This

Are you ready? You can do this! Acknowledge. Confess. Be forgiven. And come out from hiding. You don't have to make a public confession or post on social media. But I want to encourage you to start by acknowledging the very thing that is producing your shame. Get a journal and confess it to the Lord. He can handle whatever you have to bring to Him. And if it makes it any easier for you, He already knows about it. After you have confessed it, know that He has forgiven you of it. You must believe that. I would also encourage you to find a trusted friend to confess to. First John 1:9 says, "If we confess our sins, he is faithful and just to forgive us our sins and to cleanse us from all unrighteousness." Find a person you trust and share these things. I promise you, there is freedom and rest on the other side of this. *"There is therefore no condemnation for those who are in Christ Jesus."*

Questions for Reflection

1. Have you acknowledged the sin producing shame?

2. Have you confessed it to God? If not, why not?

3. Who is a safe person you can confess to? When will you confess?

"He Covers Your Shame"

⌒

CHAPTER 2

Battle

*A Hostile Encounter or Engagement
between Opposing Military Forces*

The mind is a powerful battlefield. It's where hopes and dreams live or die. And where the truth struggles to stay alive.

A hostile encounter between two powerful forces is always taking place in our minds. The battle is between thinking thoughts that are good, true, and noble and giving in to those that are self-deprecating and untruthful. It's hand-to-hand combat between truths and lies. It's a battle we will all face and a battle we must be prepared to fight. It starts at an early age and continues until the day we take our last breath. It's a battle we all have in common: everyone from a young child to a mature adult can understand what it means to wage war with our thoughts.

A Cornell University study revealed that the average person has between twelve thousand and sixty thousand thoughts per day. Of those thousands of thoughts, 80 percent are negative, and 95 percent are repeated thoughts from the day before— meaning most of us think the same negative thoughts over and over again.[1] This is a defeating reality! Boys and girls are growing up quickly, having to learn how to fight their thoughts at an early age. Teens and college students are in mental battles desperately trying to find the power to continue fighting each day. And adults have been engaged in this battle for as long as they can remember, but they haven't discovered the secret to winning.

> A hostile encounter between two powerful forces is always taking place in our minds.

Negative thoughts and lies are a powerful army that never enters a cease-fire. The mental artillery keeps coming at us and has no regard for the flag of surrender we wave. The battle seems impossible to win. These two opposing powerful forces have the ability to give life or take it. And this is just for the average person.

But what about the person who not only has to deal with the negative thoughts on repeat but also experienced life trauma and deals with mental illness? People like this probably feel like they don't stand a chance in this battle and find it easier to live in defeat. These people probably feel like they are on a battlefield with their thoughts and no one is there to defend them or fight with them. They are prisoners of war and have declared defeat on themselves because it's all they have ever known.

The battlefield is never a fair fight, and the assaults of the enemy have no mercy on those who struggle with mental illness or any other mentally debilitating trauma. Mental illness has declared war on many people, and the results of this war are devastating. Just consider the following statistics:

- Depression is the leading cause of disability in Americans ages fifteen to forty-four.
- Depression is the number 3 workplace issue in the U.S.
- Suicide is the number 2 leading cause of deaths in the U.S for ages fifteen to forty-four.

- Around 250,000 Americans survive suicide annually.
- There is one suicide death every twelve minutes in the U.S.
- As many people in America die from suicide as breast cancer.
- Around 50,000 people died from suicide last year.[2]

According to these statistics, we are in a losing battle. And it's ruining lives. Negativity and lies have taken residency in our minds, and it's time to take back our mental battleground.

My Mess: The Battle

If you could peel back the layers and enter my mind, you would find that it's filled with mental wounds and scars from the battle that has been ongoing for years. I have never really had the mental training to win many battles. My strategy was weak and feeble, and my artillery never disarmed the enemy. I typically found myself losing the fight and giving in to self-deprecating thoughts and untruths about myself. Years of constantly losing caused me to give up and settle for the fact that becoming a prisoner to my thoughts was easier than being a free man.

These mental battles are exhausting. Having to decipher truths from lies and discern what voice is God's, mine, or the enemy's is a heavy mental burden to carry. As soon as I woke up, my mind began to prepare itself for the war that lay ahead. Leftover lies from the day before still lingered in my mind and distorted my perspective, leaving me paralyzed. My thoughts consumed me and affected every decision I made each day.

It often seemed like every time I took a step forward to live in what God had called me to, I regressed and found myself believing those same old lies of the enemy. I looked in the mirror and saw a distorted vision of myself. All I could see was a prisoner who was mentally chained to the lies. My mind blocked me from seeing a clear view of who God had created me to be. I became mentally shackled.

If you are anything like me, then you know truth struggles to stay alive. True thoughts have a short life span. But the lies on the other hand have learned to set up post and become long, faithful residents. It's a battle against a powerful

> True thoughts have a short life span.

enemy: lies, trauma, and mental illness. I have waived the flag in surrender, but there wasn't a foxhole deep enough to protect me from my thoughts.

Several battles are typically going on in my mind on any given day: what "they" say about me, what I say about myself, mental illness, and what God says. I know that's a lot to sift through.

Battle 1: What "They" Say about Me

We can all remember impactful things that were said to us—words that were life-giving and birthed a new-found hope in us as well as words that were hurtful and broke our spirit. Our brains have the power and capacity to keep all these words stored.

I was a raised in a thick-skinned Hispanic culture. Verbal abuse was common and one of many ways to discipline children. This kind of abuse was a way to mentally break down a child so they wouldn't dare challenge the person in authority. Demeaning one another was second nature, and nothing was out of bounds. I was called everything—an idiot, stupid, dumb, a wimp, with a whole bunch of expletives thrown in. The list could go on.

The words hurt in the moment, but I brushed them off and buried them deep. I had no clue that the words planted in my mind at a young age would produce rotten fruit in my life as an adult. These words were like land mines being planted in my brain that would activate with the slightest pressure throughout the rest of my life. So, when someone speaks a negative word about me, they don't realize that they are activating a mental land mine that was placed in my mind when I was a young child.

Years later those words still echo in my mind. I still battle with hearing and thinking that I am not enough. Not smart enough. Not man enough. Not enough! The war is still real, and the battle hasn't subsided.

I know you may be thinking I just need to get over it and move on. I agree, but it's not that easy for me. And my guess is, it's not that easy for you either.

We have all heard the childhood response to destructive words, "Sticks and stones may hurt my bones, but words will never hurt me." Well, that's far from the truth. Words hurt, they crush, and they can be used by the enemy. We have all had things said about us that have crushed our souls. It hurts deeply, especially when it's by those we have let into our circle of trust. We replay those things over and over in our minds. For some of us it has been years, but those things that were said still seems so freshly engraved in our mind. They feel like a wound that never heals.

Things people say about me impact me probably more than they should. Words stay with me for hours, days, weeks, and months. Words from years ago will randomly pop back into my head, and I find myself dwelling on these untruths. I can find myself recycling thoughts and putting them on repeat. I've always been this way.

Land mines are an interesting military tactic. Research shows that the most deadly legacy of the twentieth century is the use of land mines in warfare. Land mines are explosive devices designed to trigger by pressure. They are used by military forces to disable their opponents. These land mines are hidden slightly under the surface, going undetected, and are triggered by pressure or contact. Over the years these military forces have forgotten where the land mines have been placed, and years later they still have deadly consequences. Since 1975, land mines have killed or hurt more than one million people around the world.[3]

This is what happens to us. Throughout our lives words have been planted in our minds that we haven't forgotten, and it doesn't take much to activate them. All it needs is a little bit of pressure. The artillery they shoot at us doesn't just go away when the enemy stops shooting, like a shotgun blast. It lingers and has deadly effects for years, even decades.

It's time we learn how to disarm the enemy. Keep this in mind. What *they* say may hurt us, but it doesn't change what *He* says about us. All it can do is distract us from what He says about us. I know it hurts when people say things about you, but let me encourage you. The words of men cannot thwart the plans of God. What they say about you cannot change what God has planned for you!

Battle 2: What I Say about Myself

I have the gift of self-deprecation. The things I say about myself to myself are absolutely dehumanizing. I tell myself why I can't do things. I ridicule and demean my leadership. I call myself names that I would be embarrassed for people to know about. And I am my own worst critic. No one has ever been harder on me than me. I torture myself with words and give myself verbal lashes. I create narratives in my mind that are untrue. I have the ability to take a thought and turn it into a mental novel that is filled with lies and worst-case scenarios. To be honest, I don't put up much of a fight anymore. Writing these

> No one has ever been harder on me than me.

novels has become a mental addiction. I have surrendered and am a prisoner to my thoughts. I'm a prisoner of war.

In ancient Rome, being a prisoner of war was absolutely brutal. Prisoners were brought before the Roman military leaders, and from there they would decide what to do with them. Typically, when prisoners were caught, they were tortured and used as slaves. They were subjected to their military opponent and had to do whatever that opponent wanted them to do. Sometimes this led to drowning, beatings, crucifixion, or being used as a gladiator to entertain the crowds. It was a torturous position to be in. No power, no hope, and full subjection to the enemy.

This is a metaphor for most of my life. Paul, in 2 Corinthians 10:5, says, "Take every thought captive to obey Christ," but I found my thoughts taking me captive. I became a prisoner who was being mentally tortured, and I didn't know how to break out of it. It sometimes felt easier not to put up a fight and to allow myself to learn how to function as a prisoner. The taste of victory seemed far from being a reality. I was weak and wounded, a prisoner in need of rescue.

These thoughts paralyzed my life and damaged my relationships. I demeaned myself so much that I started believing that everyone else saw me in the light that I was seeing myself. I believed I was incapable and a nobody, and I believed others thought the same about me. It was debilitating and defeating, and I couldn't hear the voice of God.

But be encouraged. This is a battle we can learn to defeat. We can renew our minds and begin to replace the negative things we think and say to ourselves with things that are true! We will get to this in a moment.

Battle 3: What Depression Says about Me

Unfortunately, my battles don't end there. I not only have to battle these negative thoughts from what others have said about me or what I say about myself, but I also have to battle what depression says about me. I have to be honest, it feels like I am having to fight these battles wounded. Having to fight what depression says about me is a daily battle, "I am not enough" "I can't do it" "I am a failure" "life will never get better." And the list goes on and on. Depression tells me I am in a funk that I can never overcome. Mental illness is a beast we cannot always pray away. Trust me, I've tried.

Years ago I found myself in a deep spiritual hole. I felt hopeless and dark within my soul. I went through an intense season of figuring out what to name this "thing" in my life. Was it spiritual warfare? Was it depression? Maybe both? Even if I could call and identify it, I still had to learn how to control it.

I remember hearing the doctor's words telling me it was depression, and I would have to be on antidepressants. I was automatically ashamed and embarrassed. I hated hearing the word *depression*. It was depressing! I felt weak, like I was somehow less of a person.

I knew there is this deeply rooted stigma attached to depression in the Christian world, especially in the church. I didn't want to fall into that category so I lived with this secret for years, afraid of being found out. I was ashamed and hated that depression found me.

> There is this deeply rooted stigma attached to depression in the Christian world, especially in the church.

The truth is, I didn't ask for depression to come my way, and depression never asked me if it could come in. That's not how this works. It just showed up, unannounced, with no invitation.

I remember hearing that people with depression should think positive thoughts. I did that, and the depression didn't go away. I heard I should memorize Scripture.

I did that, and the depression didn't go away. Nothing seemed to help, and I felt stuck.

I don't mean to be a killjoy, but this is my reality. Did I believe God could heal me? Yes. So I took the approach of desperately pleading with Him to heal me. I felt like Paul when he confessed, "Three times I pleaded with the Lord about this, that it should leave me. But he said to me, 'My grace is sufficient for you, for my power is made perfect in weakness'" (2 Cor. 12:8–9).

I remember asking God, "Why won't you heal me?" I told Him I could be a more effective husband, father, and pastor. But no answer. I became frustrated at times, even angry.

Just because God can heal doesn't necessarily mean He will . . . at least not in this life. All Christians are promised ultimate future healing at the resurrection, but until then we may walk with a limp like Jacob or be left with our weakness like Paul. Ultimately, I learned to accept this and trust that His grace is sufficient.

But this is easier to type than it is to live.

While the ups and downs of my emotions may look similar to a roller coaster at an amusement park, I have learned that the Word of God remains a constant. Even though my negative thoughts told me God left me, and this battle would never end, and I have no hope, I've learned to live a life that consistently balances my mental wars with God being my armor-bearer in the battle. It's hard, but I know it can be done.

Mental illness may be an ongoing battle for you. It is for me. But you can do it! We don't have to resign ourselves to failure. God's Word is powerful and sufficient to get you through each day. We are in a day-by-day battle. Depression has a lot to say about me, but what God has to say is greater.

Battle 4: What God Says about Me

You can start winning mental wars, but it's going to take some work. You will have to learn how to fight in order to win. You can't just surrender to the lies and accept defeat.

Lies have been swarming your mind, running and ruining your life, but it doesn't have to be that way. You do not have to be a prisoner to your thoughts! You may have been taken captive, but it's time to break free. When a prisoner of war is captured, the enemy takes the captured prisoner to their commander, and the commander decides what to do with the prisoner. In that moment they are under the authority of the enemy with absolutely no power. They are captured, chained, and submitted.

Many of us have been allowing the lies to capture us, chain us, and bring us into submission like prisoners of war. But our thoughts only have the authority we allow them to have. Lies don't stand a chance when they're brought before the right commander.

> You do not have to be a prisoner to your thoughts! You may have been taken captive, but it's time to break free.

Instead of allowing the lies to take us captive, we need to capture the lies and bring them before the right commander, God. He will decide whether they have any power or authority in our lives. You will soon realize they don't stand a chance when you bring them to the right commander. They have to be placed against the truth in order for them to lose their power and authority over you. But if you do not fight lies with the truth, then you will remain a prisoner.

The truth will set you free! God's Word is going to be the strategy and artillery you need in order to disarm and diffuse the battle of "they," "you," or the enemy.

Fight!

As Christians, we have the greatest weapons available to us: prayer, community, the Holy Spirit, and the Word of God. So, how do we fight these lies? With the truth!

Throughout Scripture, Paul gives his readers great insight into how to fight. In Philippians 4:8 he tells them to set their minds on things that are true, honorable, just, pure, and lovely. In Romans 12:2 he tells his readers to be "transformed by the renewal of your mind." In Ephesians 6:17, he speaks about "the helmet of salvation," which is protecting the mind.

In the Roman army the helmet would protect the head from an instant kill shot. This is what the enemy targets today—the mind. He knows that it can be an instant spiritual kill shot that will leave us sidelined in our despair.

We have a real enemy that opposes us and is using force to wound us and evil to kill us. One of his strategic attacks is on the mind. If he can change the way we view ourselves and the way we view God, then he knows he can win the battle. He has planted mental land mines that are filled with explosive lies and untruths, and he strategically activates them with a goal of mentally wounding and paralyzing us. He knows that if we believe these lies we won't walk in the freedom God has called us to. These lies have proven to be a winning strategy for the enemy, effective in the lives of believers.

Paul was a man who understood what it meant not only to battle thoughts of who he used to be but also to battle all that came with external persecution. In 2 Corinthians 1:8, he says that he "despaired of life itself." Paul had to learn through experience what it means to protect the mind from thoughts that are not from God.

Do you know what I've realized about this Christian walk? If I don't take my thoughts captive, they take me captive, and I become a prisoner to my mind. Eventually, my thoughts will give birth to action. It's how some of us have gotten into deep despair. Our minds took us places our feet never intended to go. Our actions became the visible image of our invisible thoughts.

> If I don't take my thoughts captive, they take me captive.

Through the years these words have explained this concept well:

> Watch your thoughts; they become
> words.
> Watch your words; they become actions.

Watch your actions; they become habits.

Watch your habits; they become
character.

Watch your character; it becomes your
destiny.[4]

Many of us have taken thoughts that are not from God and have written mental novels that were never intended to be written. Do you ever let your mind wander into places it should never go? Do you allow your mind to spend mental bandwidth on things that may not be true? If you can relate, you are not alone. I think most of us have done this, and it's exhausting.

Our minds create a false reality, and we begin to live in this made-up world. We look at people differently. We begin to question people's motives. We assume the worst. We are suspicious and don't trust anyone. How did we get to this place? I'll tell you how. Our minds wrote a fictional story that we began to live out.

This could play out in a number of ways. Maybe as a teenager, you're convinced your parents want to suck the fun out of your life. You think they don't understand what it's like to be a teen in today's world. So, when they tell you that you can't go to the party, or need to be home by a certain time, you read their actions through the lens of your assumptions about them. The *only reason* they could be telling you no, you think, is because they want to take the fun out of your life.

Or maybe you're inherently untrusting of authority. You think everyone in a position of power is corrupt. So, when your boss at work makes a decision, you don't understand, or when your pastor does something differently than you would, you think the *only reason* they could do this is because they're abusing their authority.

Or maybe it's in a friendship or with a person you're dating. You've believed the enemy's lies that you're worthless, that if anyone ever really got to know you, they wouldn't want to be around you. So, how do you respond when you hear that your best friend was hanging out with someone else and you didn't get invited? Or when your wife made a positive comment about her friend's husband? Do you get paranoid, like all the sudden you no longer have their affection or commitment?

If we are not careful, we can make some foolish decisions based on this false reality we have created. In all of these cases, you could be right, but you could also be completely wrong. Your parents probably have your best interests in mind. Your authority figure probably has access to information you don't have. Your friend or spouse is probably still completely committed to you. But when we buy into lies and let thoughts take us captive, they can poison the way we see all these situations and ruin our relationships.

So, how do you correct this? How do you start winning battles? I'll tell you how: change your strategy and weapons!

His Message: Setting Your Mind on the Spirit

In Romans 8:5–6, Paul gives us an excellent remedy for our mental battle. He gives us two clear paths: "For those who live according to the flesh set their minds on the things of the flesh, but those who live according to the Spirit set their minds on the things of the Spirit. For to set the mind on the flesh is death, but to set the mind on the Spirit is life and peace." That's a powerful statement. In other words, where you set your mind will determine whether you win or lose the battle.

This is the Christian battle. Our minds battle between the things of the flesh and the things of the Spirit. So, which one wins? According to Paul, it's the one you set your mind on. Let's take a look and see the outcome of where we put our minds.

In verse 5, Paul states, "Those who live according to the flesh set their minds on the things of the flesh." The phrase "set their minds" is one word in Greek that means "to be absorbed or to focus on something." When Paul speaks of the flesh, he is talking about things that are contrary to God's character. Although Paul is speaking about unbelievers, we must not be fooled thinking that only deeply depraved sinners set their minds on the flesh. This could easily be the Bible study teacher, the elder, the deacon, or the pastor. Believers can undoubtedly find themselves consumed with the things of the flesh.

The flesh does not want to submit to truth. So, when thoughts are contrary to God's character, not only does it displease God, but it can lead to destructive actions. Fleshly thinking can lead to fleshly actions. No one of us is exempt—this battle is for believers and unbelievers alike. Carnal thoughts, fleshly thoughts, do not want to submit to truth. That is why they keep coming back. They won't go out without a fight. They want to live!

We give these thoughts life by allowing them to take residency in our minds. Paul makes it straightforward for us. If you want to know whether you are walking in the flesh or the Spirit, check your thoughts; they will tell you. Typically, the result of a life that has its mind set on the flesh is brokenness. This is why Paul says it brings death.

According to Galatians 5, the life of someone who's mind is set on the flesh is easy to spot because it's filled with "sexual immorality, impurity, sensuality, idolatry, sorcery, enmity, strife, jealousy, fits of anger, rivalries, dissensions, divisions, envy, drunkenness, orgies, and things like these" (vv. 19–21). Did you see yourself somewhere in that list?

For the person who is not a believer in Jesus Christ, this death that is brought by the flesh is an eternity away from God. For the believer, we should no longer live a life focused on the things of the flesh but of the Spirit. Although as Christ followers we are delivered from the penalty of sin and its eternal consequences, the mind set on the flesh still brings death in the form of destructive patterns of our lives that we allow our thoughts to lead us into. We will never stop sinning and experiencing the earthly consequences of our sins, but this should not become our standard way of living.

There is a sanctification process, or setting apart, that every believer enters when we place our faith in Jesus. Our flesh, unfortunately, doesn't go away. Each of us still has a past. We all still have struggles. There is yet a battle going on. In Romans 7, Paul calls this the war within the mind.

So news flash to the Christian: *you will still struggle.* You will have thoughts that do not seem to want to go away. And you will be reminded of the things you did and the things that were done to you. You will struggle with your thoughts until God makes you whole one day. But there is a way to live in victory now. That way has to do with where we set our minds.

This is how you win the battle. You fight lies with truth. Paul says, "For to set the mind on the flesh is death, but to set the mind on the Spirit is life and peace" (Rom. 8:6). There is the key to victory. You have to replace and reject the negative thoughts or sinful thoughts with truth.

Your fleshly thoughts are contrary to God's character; defeat them with the truth of God. If the enemy reminds you of your past, then focus on Scriptures about forgiveness. Reach into your armory—the Word of God—and pull out the weapons of truth that will defuse any degrading and demeaning thoughts. When my mind is not focused and set on Scripture, I will not be able to defeat the thoughts contrary to what God says. When my mind is focused on Scripture, I have what I need to take every thought captive.

Christians, we must set our minds on the things of the Spirit because those things bring life and peace. Your reality remains true, but the difference is you now see with a new perspective. You see your sin and know you are forgiven. You can take the traumatic experiences and know that what the enemy intended for harm, God can use for good. You no longer look at your life through the lens of condemnation and destruction, but instead you look through the lens of life and peace. This life is the eternal destiny that can never be taken away from you, and this peace is the peace you have with God that no one can steal!

Questions for Reflection

1. What are some lies you are believing?

2. Are your thoughts consistent with fleshly thoughts or Spirit thoughts?

3. What Bible verses should you memorize to help you walk by the Spirit rather than the flesh?

"What They Say about You Cannot Change What God Has Planned for You"

CHAPTER 3

⌒

Philophobia

The Fear of Love or Being Loved

*H*ow could anyone ever love me? This was the question that haunted me for most of my life. I genuinely believed I was unworthy of love. I was too dirty, too broken, too shattered to be loved.

The word *love* was attached to pain. Love, for me, wasn't a word that brought positive emotions. I didn't think of a Disney fairy tale or a movie that ended in warm or fuzzy feelings. The complete opposite plagued me; I was tormented with the overwhelming fear of love.

Love, for me, meant hurt, brokenness, pain, and betrayal. Love was a word I wanted to hide from, and I questioned its existence.

I'm going to enter a transparent time with you to understand a little better the depths of my shattered soul.

I want you to hear how damaged I was and why love for me was so hard to receive and give. But I also want you to see how the gospel took a word I despised and turned it into a word I hide in. Ready? Here we go.

My Mess: A Wall Began to Build

Love for me was shattered at an early age. I will never forget the sounds and images I saw as a young boy. Dishes being thrown against the wall and drunken degrading slurs to my mother were daily occurrences in our household.

My father worked odd jobs and continued to drink. My mother became the primary provider and worked long and hard hours. When my mother was gone, I was a bit of a Lone Ranger. I would hop on my bike and travel the streets, seeing what kind of adventure I could get into. My brother and I would ride our bikes and go into a pretend world. We would play for hours. We would turn into an episode of *Chips*—two police officers with California swag who chased the bad guys. I became Erik Estrada (the cool guy with a lot of swag), and my brother became Larry Wilcox (his level-headed partner). We set our sights on catching the bad guys.

This became an escape from my reality. It gave me space to breathe. But even though I was safe on the streets playing a police officer, I still wasn't safe in the walls of my own home. Little did I know how much more my six-year-old soul was about to experience. There was a young soul that was about to be shattered beyond repair.

Sexual Abuse

Hispanic culture emphasizes family and hospitality. Weekend barbecues are a typical occasion. We stayed the night at family members' homes on a weekly basis. But at five years old, I was left at the wrong house.

This would be the mallet that shattered any piece of my soul I felt was left. A family member molested me. It was supposed to be a safe place. They were supposed to watch me and protect me but instead preyed on my innocence and took the only pure thing I had left in me, my sexuality.

From this point on, I fought and never told anyone what I was fighting. This wouldn't be the last family member who would try to molest me. I found myself running with nowhere to hide and no one to protect me. My soul was being destroyed, and I was too young to understand the pain and shame I experienced. I didn't trust anyone. Not one person. Love was attached to hurt, pain, and betrayal. Anger and rage took over my heart, and I became a rebellious kid who starved to be the center of attention, desperately trying to repair the shattered pieces of my heart. I felt too dirty to be loved so I decided to accept that as my reality and take a path of destruction. My sexually purity was stolen from me and continued to be less and less sacred. When I was seven years old, family members sat me down and introduced me to pornography. I will never forget the laughing that went on as I watched in terror of what I was seeing. By the fifth grade I was dabbling in sexual immorality. And by the time I was in high school, any and all conviction was completely gone.

> Anger and rage took over my heart, and I became a rebellious kid who starved to be the center of attention, desperately trying to repair the shattered pieces of my heart.

I did it for fulfillment and repair, but it was all just an empty attempt to be whole again.

In this picture, you see a young boy with a big smile, but behind that smile was a tormented soul being held by the chains of pure evil. More bricks were laid, and the wall continued to build.

A Wall That Will Never Be Broken

Shortly after that experience, my parents ended up separating and eventually getting a divorce. I will get into this in a later chapter, but this became my breaking point.

The hurt turned into anger. The anger turned into actions. I became numb and bitter toward the world. I was determined never to let anyone ever hurt me again. I vowed to myself that no one would ever get close enough to hurt me, so I put walls up that were so high and thick they eventually became unbreakable.

You Can't Get Through!

By the time I was a young adult, I had left a trail of broken relationships. Relationships that I intentionally ruined before they ruined me. I was highly dysfunctional in my relational approach and ended up hurting a lot of people. My mentality became, "Hurt them before they hurt me."

I would put people through trial runs to see how long they would stay. I was mean, short-tempered, and hard to love. The closer someone got to breaking down the walls I set up, the harder I would push to see if they would stay. In my mind, if they remained after all of the hell I put them through, then they loved me. If they left, then they didn't. It was impossible for me to love or to risk having others love me.

I didn't know how to allow someone to love me for me. I didn't know how to love someone for them. I struggled with philophobia, the fear of loving and being loved. Love was something I didn't want to experience if it meant pain. Protecting myself from experiencing pain, again, was my main priority. I learned to set up a brick wall that could never be broken. On the outside I was firm, confident, and tough. But on the inside I was still a five-year-old boy who yearned for affirmation, nourishment, and unconditional love. This feeling eventually left me looking for love in all the wrong places.

Unfortunately, I may not be the only one who understands what this is like. In 2015, 670,000 children spent time in U.S. foster care. On any given day at least 400,000 children are in foster care.[1] These numbers are staggering.

Simultaneously, many great organizations are fighting to lower this number by finding a loving family to place these children. I can't help but wonder how many of these children will struggle with love. I can't help but wonder how many of these children will place walls up because they are afraid of love. How many of these children question the love of God? And how many question His very existence?

How many will be like me and believe the enemy's lie, that God doesn't love them?

His Message: The Love of God Adopts Us

In Romans 8, Paul gives us a breathtaking view of God's love. He uses a phrase that would hit the core of the Roman culture, "Spirit of adoption." "For you did not receive the spirit of slavery to fall back into fear, but you have received the *Spirit of adoption* as sons, by whom we cry, 'Abba! Father!'" (Rom. 8:15, emphasis added).

If a family in the Roman culture had a child they no longer wanted, they would go to a far-off community and leave the child in the street like a stray animal. The streets were flooded with hundreds of orphans. Could you imagine that? Your family not wanting you, so they dropped you off in an unknown city and sped off, never to be seen again? The brokenness the children experienced had to be unbearable. For the ones lucky enough not to die after being abandoned, the healing and restoring of trust had to be a lifelong process. What did these children do to deserve such a thing? Nothing. Absolutely nothing at all.

In this culture everyone desired to have a male child to have someone to leave their inheritance to. They wanted someone to carry on their legacy and be the heir of their possessions. The wealthy would often go into Rome to find an orphan who could be the heir of the family. It could be a male of any age.

So picture this. A man is searching the streets for a child who is more than likely filled from head to toe with dirt-road filth. The child has probably made poor choices to survive the mean streets of Rome. He has done things he is ashamed of. His heart is hard. He feels unloved and unworthy of love. His soul is completely shattered beyond repair. But it all changes because a soon-to-be father is motivated by love and pursues this child with a shattered soul.

The soon-to-be father sets his eyes on the child and says, "This one, this is the one I choose to lavish my love on. This is the one I choose to be an heir of my possessions." What a picture! The child didn't have to go clean himself up first. He didn't have to have a track record of moral purity. He didn't have to dress up or interview for the father's love. He had nothing to offer. What did he do to deserve it? Nothing. It was all motived by the father's initiative.

This is the picture Paul is trying to paint. We were orphans who had absolutely nothing but filthy rags to offer our father, but He, motivated by love, chose us.

Now you might be thinking, *The father was still motivated by some level of selfishness. After all, he was looking for an heir.* And you might be right. But that's why our story, being adopted by God, is even better. We have nothing to add to God. God doesn't need an heir to carry on His legacy. We can't give God anything He doesn't already have. So what must His motivation be in adopting us? Nothing but pure love and grace and mercy! God loves us and adopts us, even though we have nothing to give back to Him!

Once the father chose the child off Rome's streets, there was typically a process that took place to make it official. First, there was a legal transaction. As soon as the father signed the documents to make it official, any debt in the past and the child's future would have been accrued by the father. So the father was not only saying to the courts that he would take full responsibility for any debt in the past but that he would also take on any debt the child occurred in the future. Can you imagine that? The child is sitting there feeling unloved, has trust issues, knows that he will do dumb things in the future, and his new dad is saying, "I got it all covered."

The next step in the process would be an instant name change. Just as the name was changed, the child now became heir of all the father had. The child didn't have to prove himself before becoming an heir. His rights didn't have to outweigh his wrongs. The only prerequisite was a new name, given by the father.

Now the child wasn't entirely free to live irresponsibly but instead had new obligations. The child no longer had to live in the streets. No more crimes had to be committed for survival—no more hungry nights. Provision was going to be taken care of. Now he had a new role to play. He had to choose to leave his old life behind and now aim to live and please his father. His new aim was to honor his father and abstain from the things that pained him.

Let's pause for a minute. What a picture Paul gave us of adoption. He paints the love of a heavenly father so well for the readers. A father who pursues the orphan who has nothing to offer but filthy rags. He takes all debt— past, present, and future. The father then gives him the privilege of being an heir of all his possessions. What a marvelous picture of God's pursuing and agape love for all of humanity!

Without Christ we are orphans. We had nothing but filthy rags to offer God, yet He pursued us with a love that would cover all we had ever done and will ever do. We didn't have to interview or perform for this kind of love. We don't even have to perform to keep it. It will never leave us!

Is it hard for you to believe this? Does it almost seem too good to be true? Can you genuinely believe that God loves you? Or do you have trouble processing that reality?

I can relate to all of the above, but I am glad to say I'm learning every day what it means to love and be loved by my heavenly Father. He has been so patient with me, even in the moments when I tried to push Him away to see if He would stay. He has proven Himself faithful even when I have been found unfaithful, and He will do the same for you.

After the legal transaction has been made before the courts of heaven and we have been adopted by God the Father through Christ, there are several implications for us.

> I'm learning every day what it means to love and be loved by my heavenly Father.

The Love of God Leads Us

The first thing that happens is we automatically became His child. In verse 14, Paul says that the Spirit of God now leads sons of God (those who accepted Christ). We are no longer on the streets like orphans without direction, but now we are set into a family with a father who is always leading and guiding us. The Spirit who leads us is God's deposit and promise that lets us know we belong to Him. The Spirit will lead us, convict us, and, most importantly, will never leave us. It's like having an internal GPS that always leads us in the right direction. There will be times as children when we will fall and disobey, and the internal GPS (the Spirit) will say, "Wrong turn, take a left." He will keep speaking to you until you correct your course.

A GPS will not shut off because you aren't listening, and neither does the Spirit. The Spirit will always tell us when we are taking a wrong turn and kindly convict us to correct the course. He will never be quiet and let us live in peace. There is no turning Him off, and He will not leave us.

As miserable as this can be, it is a sure sign we belong to Him. Because we no longer have to live this life, clueless as to where to turn. This kind of love from God is hard to understand. But let me tell you something: you can be filled with intentional wrong turns in your life, and He will never stop loving you. His desire to lead you is motivated by His love for you. He will not leave you like a father or mother who left their child behind. He will not drop you off in the streets like the orphans in the Roman culture.

Paul uses the most intimate word that he can use in verse 15: "Abba." We only see this word used three times in the New Testament. It is the most intimate word that could be used, and it means dad or daddy. It's intimacy right now at this moment. Not later but now. This is an Aramaic word that is first used in the New Testament by Jesus. This word was bothersome for a lot of Jews. They felt like God was so holy that He couldn't be seen as an intimate father. When Paul uses this word, he brings a new revelation to who God is in a way that seems like heresy to many. He reveals this hidden truth that because of Christ we can be so intimately acquainted with this God who knows every little detail about our lives and still loves us. We can call Him daddy.

Many people in your life may not have stayed around when your flaws were exposed. Your father may have left you at an early age. You may have gone through a divorce. You may feel like the loneliest person alive. But Paul tells us that we have a God who is willing to be our daddy. A God who knows all and is never going to leave us, unfriend us, or divorce us. He is a Father who is here to stay.

The Love of God Affirms Us

Growing up with an absent father led me to create an idol of affirmation. I did anything and everything I needed to do to be affirmed by those around me. In school I became the class clown. In sports I tried to be the best. This search to fill an idol of affirmation took me from drinking to drugs. All in search of affirmation.

We all want to be affirmed. We want something that makes us feel valuable, essential, and gives us purpose. We work tirelessly to obtain this. We work hard for a promotion. We desperately want to be somebody of importance. If we pause long enough to search deep enough, we realize that all of our efforts are an empty attempt to fill a void of assurance. We look to our spouses. Our supervisors. Our pastors. And in the end we are frustrated because we feel like no one is affirming us the way we believe we deserve to be. We end up chasing an idol we will never be able to catch. The idol of affirmation was never meant to be caught.

In Romans 8:16, Paul says, "The Spirit himself bears witness with our spirit that we are children of God." Paul says that now that we are children of God, the Spirit will continuously affirm us that we are loved. Doesn't that blow your mind? For most of my life, I starved for the love and affections of someone, anyone who wouldn't hurt me. I wanted to be affirmed! And now Paul is saying that God wants to do that for me. The God of the heavens. The Creator of the universe wants to continuously demonstrate that He loves me and isn't going anywhere! He will stand and testify on our behalf. We now have a protector who will affirm His love for us, and one way He will do that is by standing up for us to testify that we are His! Whoa! Oh, but wait, there's more. For me, being loved and affirmed probably would be enough. But Paul doesn't stop there.

> We all want to be affirmed.

The Love of God Makes Us Coheirs with Christ

Paul continues describing this incomprehensible kind of love. In verse 17, he opens the floodgates. He says that "if [we are] children, then [we are] heirs—heirs of God and fellow heirs with Christ."

What?

Let's chew on this for a minute. As if loving us and accepting us weren't enough, now God is saying, "By the way, because of this legal transaction, being a child means you get what I have." And what God has for us is secure, safe, and no one can ever take it away. You will never lose it!

I am a big fan of the show *Undercover Boss*. The CEO of a large organization will go undercover and try to discover where the company can improve. While doing this, the undercover boss is partnered with an employee, and the CEO uses this time to ask questions that will reveal the employee's heart toward the company. These conversations usually lead to some brutal truths about the company but typically take a turn where the employee spills their heart out to the undercover boss.

My favorite part is always the end of the show. The boss reveals to the employees their true identity. After talking about areas the organization needs to improve, the boss makes a generous statement. He or she lavishes gift after gift on the employee. It starts with a small gift and usually gets bigger and bigger, and the employee can't believe what's happening. You can tell that if the undercover boss had stopped at the first gift, the employee would have been extremely thankful, but the boss keeps going. They lavish the employee with gifts. The employee always gets overcome with emotions, and tears begin flooding. That's usually when the tears start for me as well!

This is what it's like with God. It would have been enough if He forgave and affirmed us. But He didn't stop there. Instead, He decided to lavish us with gift after gift. Grace upon grace. What a mighty God we have!

> Surrendering and allowing God to adopt me and repurpose the ugliest parts of my life has been the best decision I have ever made.

I indeed felt like God didn't love me and wasn't for me. I experienced a lot of pain and heartache from the sexual abuse I experienced. I thought I was ruined, too disgusting to have value. But I was wrong. Surrendering and allowing God to adopt me and repurpose the ugliest parts of my life has been the best decision I have ever made. You may not feel loved. You may have a shattered soul. But let this passage of truth transform the way you see and feel God's love for you. He loves you, and just as the orphans in Rome were pursued, God pursues you!

Questions for Reflection

1. What does the word *love* mean? What has been your association with this word based on your life experiences?

2. What areas about yourself have you found hard to love?

3. Do you believe God loves you? Why or why not? Tell Him about it.

"You Are Not Too Dirty to Be Loved"

CHAPTER 4

Suffering

The State of Undergoing Pain, Distress, or Hardship

No one enjoys suffering. Yet no one can escape suffering.

All of us understand that suffering comes in unexpectedly and stays as long as it wants. It never knocks or gives us time to prepare for its grand entry; it just comes. It comes in the middle of a momentous occasion, a celebration, or in the most peaceful times of our lives. No one can ever truly prepare for the cancer diagnosis, the loss of a loved one, or mental illness. Suffering comes like a tsunami that overtakes us and throws us to and fro. It leaves a devastating trail of destruction. It takes us to a deep and dark place where hope seems foreign and pain is the new normal. Its purpose is to get us to our breaking point where we realize we have absolutely no control of the damage it causes. It attacks mentally, spiritually, physically, and emotionally.

Suffering feels like an anchor attached to our soul that's continually weighing us down, slowing down our progress in life. For some it shows up in mental instability. For others it may be physical suffering—a disease, diagnosis, or disorder. Then there are those who are continually suffering as a result of their poor decision making. Whatever side of the spectrum you sit on, I will tell you now: you can't escape suffering. It's part of living in this broken world, a by-product of the depravity of humanity.

You may not want to hear this, but you will suffer. It's unavoidable.

You can't escape suffering.

Christianity and suffering go hand in hand. To be a Christian is to enter the school of suffering. To say yes to Christ is to say yes to suffering. It's allowed by God and sometimes ordained by God. Yes, you read that correctly. God ordains suffering.

How can this be?, you think. *Doesn't God only want what's good for His children?* Yes, He does. But only He knows how to bring about what's good for His children, and sometimes that's through suffering.

Want proof? God ordained suffering for His own Son, Jesus Christ. And that suffering brought about the salvation of the world.

God ordained suffering for Jesus, and you don't have to look very hard in Scripture to find faithful saints who suffered. Joseph suffered from pain and betrayal. Job suffered through the loss of family members. Naomi lost her husband, then both of her sons. Moses was continually criticized by those he led. Elijah suffered mentally. And Paul experienced everything from physical to emotional suffering. Listen to what he says he experienced:

> Are they servants of Christ? I am a better
> one—I am talking like a madman—with
> far greater labors, far more imprisonments,
> with countless beatings, and often near
> death. Five times I received at the hands
> of the Jews the forty lashes less one. Three
> times I was beaten with rods. Once I was
> stoned. Three times I was shipwrecked;
> a night and a day I was adrift at sea; on
> frequent journeys, in danger from rivers,
> danger from robbers, danger from my

own people, danger from Gentiles, danger in the city, danger in the wilderness, danger at sea, danger from false brothers; in toil and hardship, through many a sleepless night, in hunger and thirst, often without food, in cold and exposure. And, apart from other things, there is the daily pressure on me of my anxiety for all the churches. (2 Cor. 11:23–28)

Did you read all of that? Talk about hardship! Then to add to this, he says that he despaired of life itself (2 Cor. 1:8). Did you get that?

The apostle Paul despaired of life itself.

The word *despair* means he renounced all hope. He was destitute of resources and was utterly at a loss. He had nothing to give him hope. He hated life and didn't even want to live anymore. That's a tough place to be in and a place many of us can probably relate to.

My Mess: I'm Tired of Suffering

I am not Jesus, Paul, or any of the other saints in Scripture that suffered. But I will tell you, I do understand physical, emotional, and mental suffering.

I have suffered emotionally because of the horrific things I endured as a young child. Now as an adult, I am still having to navigate that trauma. When depression knocked on my door and stayed as long as it wanted, my mental state suffered. And when I was diagnosed with an autoimmune disorder that has affected my way of living, I suffered. I don't know if God allowed it or ordained it, but I know it's here.

Suffering has taken me to the place in my life where I felt I couldn't take any more. To be completely transparent, I didn't mind if Jesus took me home. I know what it's like to pray with desperation in the midst of my suffering but feel like the prayers aren't going past my ceiling. It is complete torture to think that I am being as faithful as I can be to God, but He is completely silent.

C. S. Lewis talked about this feeling in his book *A Grief Observed*. He wrote it after his wife died and he was wrestling with the feeling that God was silent in his suffering:

> When you are happy, so happy you have
> no sense of need Him, so happy that
> you are tempted to feel His claims upon
> you as an interruption, if you remember
> yourself and turn to Him with gratitude

and praise, you will be—or so it feels—welcomed with open arms. But go to Him when your need is desperate, when all other help is vain, and what do you find? A door slammed in your faced, and a sound of bolting and double bolting on the inside. After that, silence.[1]

It's defeating to feel God has left you in the middle of your suffering. Jesus Himself experienced this when He cried out, "My God, my God, why have you forsaken me?" (Matt. 27:46). If you haven't already, you will enter a season where you cry out those same words.

Some of you have experienced the loss of a loved one, and the day you lost them haunts you every year. You dread that day.

Others are haunted by the things that were done to you as a child. Emotionally and mentally, you are in bondage to those memories.

For others, you have prayed away your depression and anxiety, and your prayers don't seem to pass the ceiling, and all you are left with is silence and mental suffering.

Then some of you are going through physical suffering. A diagnosis has shattered the way you live, and you are reminded of it every day.

No matter what category you fall into, we can all agree that suffering is hard.

Now where in the world is God in all of this suffering? Why would He allow suffering to happen to people He loves? Is He going to reward us based on the degree of our suffering? I ask this question often.

I am a faithful follower of Christ and have taken giant steps of obedience for Him, and it seems like He hasn't shielded me from any of the pain. If I am candid, sometimes I feel like I haven't received the proper compensation for my suffering. It makes me angry, bitter, and doubtful about who He is. I had often felt precisely like the psalmist: "When my soul was embittered, when I was pricked in heart, I was brutish and ignorant; I was like a beast toward you" (Ps. 73:21–22).

I am embarrassed to write this, but I can relate. There have been times in my life when my heart turned toward God. The suffering became too much, and my heart became angry. I became embittered that my faithfulness didn't lead to the same success as those around me. Instead, I was dealing with the pain of losing a child. The problem of mental illness. The pain of a broken family. Where was God? Where was my reward for my suffering? I found myself yelling at Him and sometimes cursing His name. There were even times when I intentionally disobeyed Him because I was so angry. That was hard to admit, but that's how broken and empty my soul was due to my suffering. I hated that He saw me hurting and He didn't help me.

My view on suffering became distorted due to the prosperity gospel I allowed to influence my theology. The prosperity gospel says that God rewards us for our faith, brings health and wealth, and protects us from a hard life. When this wasn't happening for me, I felt like I had held up my end of the bargain but God hadn't held up His.

That's why I took all of this so hard. Don't get me wrong: suffering is hard no matter what theology you have, but there is a great danger in a distorted view of suffering because it brings a distorted view of God. As the psalmist says, it can turn us into a brute before God.

His Message: God Hasn't Forsaken You

In Romans 8:18, Paul says that he considered "that the sufferings of this present time are not worth comparing with the glory that is to be revealed to us." He doesn't say that suffering will not happen. He doesn't sugarcoat it, promising that God rewards you on earth with something great. Instead, he focuses our attention on eternity. To suffer well, we must know God well. Scripture helps us do just that. It brings a proper perspective and a clear understanding of who God is in the midst of our suffering.

Did you know that the phrases "I am with you" and "I will never leave you or forsake you" are used more than one hundred times in the Bible? I wonder why this truth is in there so many times? Probably because God knows we continuously need to be reminded

> To suffer well, we must know God well.

of that truth! He knows we experience deep pain and suffering in this broken world. He isn't surprised when we find ourselves questioning His love for us.

We have all been at the place where it feels like God has left us to fend for ourselves. You haven't heard from Him in days, months, and even years. Reading the Bible brings frustration because it doesn't touch your soul as it once did. Listening to worship songs draws out the skeptic in you because what you once sang about, you now doubt. Your heart has hardened, and you aren't sure if things will get better. Church services (if you're still attending) seem empty and void. No sermon or pep talk can cheer up your forsaken soul.

Ever been there?

Have you ever been to the place in your life where it feels like God has left every area deserted? You are not alone. It's part of the Christian life.

When you read the theologians we deeply respect, they too went through these struggles with God. There were feelings of abandonment and great distance. From Martin Luther to Charles Spurgeon to C. S. Lewis, they all had seasons of feeling spiritually forsaken. The psalms, too, are flooded with real and raw emotions of feeling abandoned.

> As a deer pants for flowing streams, so pants my soul for you, O God. My soul thirsts for God, for the living God. When shall I come and appear before God? My tears have been my food day and night, while they say to me all the day long, "Where is you God?" (Ps. 42:1–3)

> O God, do not keep silence; do not hold your peace or be still, O God! (Ps. 83:1)

> Look to the right and see: there is none who takes notice of me; no refuge remains to me; no one cares for my soul. (Ps. 142:4)

And we can't forget about Jesus, our sweet Savior, the Son of God. In Matthew 27:46, He says the words, "My God, my God, why have you forsaken me?" Yes, even He has felt this.

So let me say to you, "Welcome to the club of feeling forsaken by God."

I know this doesn't seem like the dose you need to keep fighting, but it is! To know that we are not alone in this battle of feeling forsaken by God is encouraging. Suffering is part of the school of sanctification. Every believer will walk the road of pain and suffering.

But let me reassure you: feeling forsaken is not the same as *being* forsaken. God is a God of His Word, and He will not forsake you, no matter how you feel. Your emotions will tell you that He has gone, but the truth will remind you that He never left.

> Feeling forsaken
> is not the same as
> *being* forsaken.

Don't let your emotions dictate the truth; let the truth dictate your emotions!

God Is Not Punishing You

When life gets hard, the easy thing to believe is that it's hard because of our sin.

Growing up, I remember hearing, "God is going to punish you." It was used as a scare tactic to keep me from making the wrong decision. It didn't work, but it did form this view of God that would be hard to break.

I began to see God as a God who was angry and would jump at the opportunity to punish me when I did something wrong. When suffering entered my life, I began to replay my sins and shortcomings of the past that I thought may have caused it. I almost felt like God was paying me back. He became a God of karma. It's like He packaged His punishment toward me in different ways. For example, I thought the loss of our child might have been due to the lack of obedience to Him in the past. When I was in a car accident, I thought He was punishing me for something. It was a messed-up way of thinking, but it was the theology I had.

I know I am not alone in this thinking, but I have great news: God doesn't work this way.

You won't find it in Scripture.

It may be a good scare tactic to get children to obey their parents, but you won't find it in the Bible.

Now I do want to be clear: sin has consequences. Sometimes our suffering is a direct result of something we have done. If you steal from the store and get caught, then you get arrested. But you don't have to worry about God punishing you and giving you cancer because you stole. If you lie, then the consequence is a damaged character and mistrust, not a car accident.

When our emotional tank is empty, and our present circumstances don't bend in our favor, a deeply rooted insecurity may tell us God has left us because of our sin. Praise God that this isn't true! As a child of God, nothing you can do is going to run Him off. You aren't bad enough to make Him stop loving you! If life is hard right now, it's not because God is punishing you. It may be due to

> As a child of God,
> nothing you can
> do is going to
> run Him off.

your decision making or the brokenness of this world that affects you, but it's not God with this hammer in heaven who is eager to strike you and hurt you. He loves you. He may discipline us, but He is not punishing us for our sin. He punished Jesus for our sin; He's not going to punish us too! Praise God!

God Doesn't Owe You

This next sentence may be hard to read for some of you, but God doesn't owe us for our suffering.

I can remember many nights lying in bed, wondering how to make it all go away. I wanted to wake up and have everything magically disappear. I wanted a better life. I liked what my friends had: a mom and dad who weren't divorced. I tried to erase the things that happened to me as a child. I wanted my biological father to be back in the picture. But of course, life doesn't work that way.

On some of those restless nights, I would scroll through the channels and find myself stopping to listen to the preacher on television. I would watch it for hours. I think it was more out of curiosity than anything else. Or maybe I was looking for an answer to problems. I'm not sure exactly what it was, but it certainly intrigued me.

My life was filled with brokenness, and I wanted to exchange it for something better. Statements like, "Your life is going to get better" or "I see a financial increase coming your way" sounded appetizing for a young man who was depressed and hopeless. I felt like my soul was suffering, and I was hungry for anything to fill it. So it wasn't surprising when I latched on to the preacher selling a product that would make all of life's problems go away.

It seemed pretty simple. All I had to do is receive the product, and everything would get better. All the pain would be gone, and I would be on the path to a better life! Over the years I continued listening to those sermons. I occasionally watched sermon clips that showed people being healed, delivered, and financially prospering! This slowly began to shape my theology. It was so appealing to me. If I could have some of that, then it would make all of the pain make sense.

The things I saw on television gave me the impression that these people were compensated for their faith and rewarded for their suffering. A piece of me wanted to experience that part of God. The part that makes things better! I wanted compensation! I felt like He owed me big time for the things I have endured.

When I gave my life to Christ, I was filled with excitement, and I anticipated the blessings that would soon fill my life. I sat back and waited for God to put the compensation plan in motion.

In my first year of following Christ, life was good. I left the old junk and sins behind and began living a morally better life. I waited tables six days a week and fought against the temptations that came my way. I enrolled in school, paid my bills, and even started a savings account. My moral track record was close to perfect, and I was confident God would bless me with good things in the future. How could He not?

Everyone was talking about my life change and could see the moral difference. Church youth groups began inviting me to share my testimony. I walked around with a Christian swag, believing I was something special and deemed for greatness. This whole Christian thing was going precisely like the televangelist said it would—Christ was making my life better. My ego was full, but God would soon destroy it.

I felt like I was doing all of the right things as a Christian, yet I didn't see rewards for my faithfulness. I don't know if the payroll angel didn't get the memo, but I was an employee now, and I didn't see much being deposited in my spiritual bank account. All of my friends who weren't living for Christ seemed to be more blessed than I was. They were getting married and moving into new homes with nice cars, and here I was—faithful, single, and broke.

I didn't understand. I began questioning whether I was doing this whole Christian thing right. I declared something in the name of Jesus, sowed financial seeds, and stayed away from sin. It drove me crazy because I couldn't figure out what I was doing wrong. When were my blessings for my suffering going to arrive?

Even more troubling was the fact that some areas of my life seemed to *worsen* due to following Christ. This will sound horrible, but sometimes the old life I left behind seemed better than the life I was living for Christ. Where was God?

I didn't know then what I know now—that He was there the entire time, and He was protecting me from myself.

See, over the years, I created this image of God based on what I had heard. My idea of God was not founded on who Scripture says He is. I never dug into the Scriptures myself to know His heart because I was too busy chasing the blessings in His hand. As I began reading and studying the Bible, I realized that it was different from what I had always heard. These characters were radically obedient and experienced extreme suffering. For many of the New Testament saints, their lives ended with being beheaded and burned at the stake. Paul and Peter—the two big shots in the early church—died by being beheaded and crucified on the cross upside down. The disciple Andrew was crucified. Thomas was pierced with the spears of four soldiers. Matthew was stabbed to death. James was stoned and clubbed to death.

Get the picture?

These faithful servants didn't receive earthly blessings for their suffering. God didn't owe them anything. They considered it a joy and an honor to suffer for Christ. These truths shattered this image I had created of God. I had to reshape my theology and how I viewed God and the suffering in my life. He didn't owe me anything, and He still doesn't!

God Rewards Us for Our Suffering

I am genuinely grateful for what God has given me. I married a woman who is beautiful inside and out, I have four beautiful children, I live in a beautiful home, and I pastor a great church. Some would say I am a blessed man, and I would agree with that.

However, I am not confident that this is the reward I have received for passing the test of suffering. Why do I know this? Because I didn't always suffer well. And not only that, but I will likely suffer again in the future.

The thing I know for sure is that God has not blessed me because of me; He has blessed me in spite of me. I believe God blesses us and rewards us with things here on earth, but that shouldn't be the believer's focus. The real reward for our suffering is what God does in us and through us. An intimacy with God happens amid our suffering that only suffering can produce. It fills our souls in ways nothing else on earth can do. It stabilizes our feet on solid ground and not sinking sand. Our souls are touched by the Creator Himself, and nothing on earth can substitute for that. There have been times in my life where I was so close to God in the middle of my suffering that I felt like I needed nothing else but Him. Then there have been times in my life where I had everything I needed, but I felt so far from Him, and I felt empty. I have found that the real reward is Him and Him alone.

Not a bigger home. Not more money. Nothing more, but Christ alone.

Suffering is good for you because when you realize that Christ is all you have, you will know that Christ is all you need. Don't buy into phrases like, "You deserve it for all that you have been through" or "God must have something great planned for you if you are suffering this much" because it only perpetuates a prosperity theology. Paul lets us know that we will suffer, and we will be rewarded. The reward may not be what you think it is; it will be much better than you can comprehend.

This is why the prosperity gospel is such a horrible lie. At the root of this heresy is the belief that God is a means to an end. We worship God *so that we can get* a bigger house, a nicer car, an awesome husband or wife, great kids, a raise, or physical healing. But the Bible tells us that God is the end—He is the goal. Through Christ we get a relationship with God. And if missing out on any of those other things draws us nearer to God, it's worth it.

The prosperity gospel is not the Christian gospel. You can't believe both. Sadly, many Americans are caught up in the prosperity gospel and are preaching it around the world. That's why pastor and author John Piper writes, "It is a tragic thing that one of our greatest exports of America is the prosperity gospel. People are being destroyed by it. Christians are being weakened by it. God is being dishonored by it. And souls are perishing because of it."[2]

In Romans 8:18, Paul says, "For I consider that the sufferings of this present time are not worth comparing with the glory that is to be revealed to us." *Consider* means that he has carefully calculated everything he is going through here on earth, and it doesn't compare to the future glory! Did you get that? What you are going through now doesn't even compare to what's waiting for you.

Paul continues in verses 19–23 and lets us know that creation will be restored and the sons of God will be revealed with redeemed bodies! Can you imagine that? If you become the richest and healthiest person on earth, it still doesn't compare to what awaits us. Let me give you a little taste and a glance at it.

> Then I saw a new heaven and a new earth,
> for the first heaven and the first earth had
> passed away, and the sea was no more.
> And I saw the holy city, new Jerusalem,
> coming down out of heaven from God,
> prepared as a bride adorned for her hus-
> band. And I heard a loud voice from the
> throne saying, "Behold, the dwelling place
> of God is with man. He will dwell with
> them, and they will be his people, and
> God himself will be with them as their
> God. He will wipe away every tear from
> their eyes, and death shall be no more,
> neither shall there be mourning, nor cry-
> ing, nor pain anymore, for the former
> things have passed away." (Rev. 21:1–4)

Hallelujah! No more suffering. No more cancer. No more tears. No more losing loved ones. No more mental illness! We will be reunited in perfect peace and harmony! What on earth can beat that?

Suffer well, and remember the reward is in spite of us, not because of us.

Questions for Reflection

1. What are your current sufferings?

2. Do you trust God in the midst of your suffering?

3. Do you think your suffering is due to your disobedience? Why? What does the Bible teach about this?

"Knowing God Well Will Allow You to Suffer Well"

CHAPTER 5

~~~

Purpose

The Reason for Which Something Is Done or Created

Can you imagine living a life where pain has no purpose? A life where all of the hardship has no meaning or value? This would be defeating. What would be the point? This would be like being dropped in the middle of the ocean with no land in sight. It feels pointless to continue swimming. It's hopeless, and you are just waiting to sink.

Thankfully, life isn't like that with God. See, because of God, our pain isn't in vain—it has meaning and purpose. Believe it or not, God can give purpose to your deepest pain.

There is a deep work in our soul that can only be done through pain and suffering. God in His sovereignty sees every piece of our shattered lives and doesn't let any of it go to waste. This breaking of the soul is a lifelong process and often comes in unexpected waves. Sometimes it stays for days, months, and even years. A dark cloud sits over our souls and remains until God decides it's time to rebuild what He has allowed to be broken. He takes all of our pain and suffering and uses it for our good and His glory. Even the circumstances our finite minds can't grasp, He uses. Even in the moments when your pain is too heavy to carry, He is working for your good.

My Mess: What Good Can Come from This?

If I pause long enough to look at the pains of this world—death, murder, human sex trafficking, and the list goes on—I am baffled at how good could possibly come from this.

These are questions we may all ponder from time to time. I don't have the answers, but I have learned to trust God at His Word.

I will never forget the cold winter day in Northwest, Arkansas. My wife and I were on a much needed date. Life was incredibly busy with two children, pregnancy, and a fast-paced ministry. Unfortunately, for us to get away and go on a date was an anomaly during this season of our lives.

We were so excited to have two hours alone together. We planned to have dinner together and head to the nearest mall to do some window-shopping. Then things took a turn for the worst. After dinner, my wife began to have excruciating pains in her stomach. We were driving from the restaurant to the nearest mall, and she could barely sit up straight. I didn't want to risk it with her being pregnant, so we turned toward the hospital.

Unfortunately, we did not get there in time. The pains got worse and worse, and right there in the car, my wife miscarried our child. It was a day we will never forget— such a traumatic moment. We rushed to the emergency room, and they quickly admitted us and began to give my wife the attention she needed. There we were in tears feeling the pain of what we just experienced. All kinds of thoughts and emotions went through our minds. What did we do wrong? Was the stress of my job too much for my wife? Should we have stayed home that night? God, why would You allow this to happen to us?

The unanswered questions quickly moved our hearts to a place of bitterness. Then, as if the night were not bad enough, we were placed next to a patient who came in to be seen because she was several months pregnant and was using drugs. We can remember hearing the lady talk about her drug use, and it infuriated us. Here we were, faithful servants of the Lord doing everything right, and we lost our child. There she was, doing everything wrong, not even caring about this precious gift God was giving her. How could this happen?

For the next several months, being around anyone pregnant and celebrating was painful for us. I know that sounds selfish, but it's the truth. One person's celebration was a reminder of our loss. It felt like a big slap in the face from God, and we couldn't comprehend what good could come from this.

After years passed, we began feeling healed enough to share our traumatic experience and the pain we felt. We shared everything from our bitterness to our anger toward God. At first, we were a bit apprehensive because we didn't want people to judge us. Then we began to see something pretty special. We noticed that we weren't alone.

The number of people who have gone through similar experiences was overwhelming. I am not saying this is a good thing because losing a child is never good. But I am saying that we could see how our pain and suffering were being used to comfort others. We were able to be a picture of hope and promise. We were testimonies of people who walked through it and are now on the other side.

I can tell you story after story about how God has taken my past sufferings and used them for my good and His glory. I have even seen Him use my past sins. He uses it all and doesn't waste any of it. He takes all things and uses them. He does it in a way only He can do. We can typically look at the pain and suffering and have no idea how it can be used for good. All we can see is the negative in it because our emotions are too fresh. But give it time. God is the master at taking broken things and using them.

One of my favorite passages is Genesis 50:20. Here's my paraphrase: "What the enemy intended for harm, God will use for good."

Joseph walked a life of betrayal, false accusation, and suffering. Chapters are filled with the things he endured. In Genesis 37, Joseph had a dream from God that placed him in honor and author-ity. In his excitement he told his brothers and father, which only led him to be the victim of jealousy. We see several times in this chapter that his brothers hated him.

> What the enemy intended for harm, God will use for good.

Shortly after this dream from God was given, life took a turn for the worse. The chapter is not even over, and we already see him sold into slavery by his brothers after they changed their minds about killing him.

By chapter 39, Joseph was in charge of the household of an important person in Egypt. God was blessing him, and he was given charge over all this man—Potiphar—owned. Things were looking as good as they could for a guy who was sold into slavery. But that didn't last too long. By the end of the chapter, Joseph found himself in prison for a false accusation by Potiphar's wife.

Can you imagine receiving a dream or promise from God that you were going to be elevated to a position of status and authority, only for everything in your life to go the complete opposite direction? Scripture doesn't tell us, but I wonder if there were nights when Joseph cried out to God, wondering where He was. I wonder if he questioned how all of this was going to turn out in the end. I'm sure none of it made sense to him.

Genesis 42:21 lets us know that his soul was in great distress. I am sure he was probably wondering how all of it was going to work out in the middle of his suffering. His life didn't match the vision God had given him.

Years of pain and suffering went by, and Joseph finally saw how all of it worked together. He received the dream at age seventeen and didn't see it come to pass until the age of thirty. That's a long time to suffer and wonder where

God is. Joseph never would have written that story for his own life. He probably imagined that his path to the top would be smooth, not the way of thorns and thistles.

Yet the course God put Joseph on probably protected Joseph from himself. Some scholars would say that Joseph had a bit of arrogance to him. He was a little too proud about that dream he had as a teenager, and perhaps that's part of what rubbed his brothers the wrong way. Maybe, just maybe, the path God put him on was to rid him of any arrogance and self-sufficiency that would have destroyed him when he was at the top. It may have been a path that produced character in him, pain he needed to endure to be prepared for his calling. In other words, maybe his character had to catch up with his calling.

God has a way to accomplish His will and plan that is unimaginable to us. His plans are on paths we would have never chosen for ourselves. We want the easy route that is pain-free, but God knows exactly what we need. And it's all for our good and His glory.

In Joseph's life we get the privilege of flipping through the pages and fast-forwarding the story to see how it all ends. We can read chapter 37 and see the promise God gave him, then jump to Genesis 50 to see how it is accomplished. Unfortunately, we don't have that advantage with our lives. Some of you are in chapter 37 and are experiencing deep pain and betrayal by those you love. Others may be in a season where you are misunderstood and falsely accused. You are entrenched in deep pain, and your soul is in great distress like Joseph's was. All you are experiencing is a mind full of promise and a handful of pain. The two don't match up the vision you had for your life. You are in the middle of your story, and you can't see the ending. You are waiting for your chapter 50 verse 20 moment, to see how God intended your hard seasons for good.

Let me promise you this: this story will unfold.

See, here is what we do know about God. He keeps His word. When God gives us a promise, we can believe it and hold onto it. And we have a promise from God that Paul gives us in Romans 8:28: "And we know that for those who love God all things work together for good, for those who are called according to his purpose." God has a way of sanctifying us on earth and preparing us for heaven. This truth still rings true for the believer today.

His Message: God's Promise

Romans 8:28, "And we know that for those who love God all things work together for good, for those who are called according to his purpose."

Some of you are holding shattered pieces of your life, wondering how any of it will be used for good. Paul is about to lay a rich foundation for the believer when it comes to God working all things for good. My hope and prayer are that this next section will give you great hope and comfort amid your suffering. I want you to know that you can count on God, and He can give your pain purpose. Let's break this down and look at the profound promise Paul gives us.

> You can count on God, and He can give your pain purpose.

"All Things"

All things. *All.* Aren't you glad Paul didn't say that God works *some* things for good? Or 99 percent of the things for good? No, the Spirit intentionally placed *all things* in this passage. Yes, even the stupid mistakes we make in our lives. God has created space for our stupidity and knows how to take those things and bring good from them.

Some of you reading this are haunted by your sins and mistakes. You are constantly reminded of them, and it has defined you. You got a divorce, had an affair, or have an addiction you can't seem to overcome. Or maybe you have lived a considerably faithful life, and suffering has entered and made a mess of your life. Our mess isn't too much for Him to repair. He knows how to take our mess and turn it into a message. He has the power to make good out of bad. He can take the very thing you thought disqualified you from His love and use it for your good and His glory. Our mess into His message. You don't have to be ashamed or hide. He can make good come from it here on earth.

"For Good"

But what does Paul mean when he says "for good"? We wouldn't dare say that death and abuse are good, and neither does Paul. There is a promise in this verse that we cannot afford to miss. The promise is not that we will escape life's hardships but that they will not have the last word. The promise is that God will take all things and work them together to produce something good.

> The promise is not that we will escape life's hardships but that they will not have the last word.

It's as if He were this master chef and takes the ingredients of our life—the suffering, the sin, and even the good—and mixes them all to make something only He can produce. The word for "good" here is *agathos*. One way it is used in the Bible is to describe something useful. So, in other words, Paul is saying that when all things are for good, they are useful. The drugs and immortality I turned from can be useful, used by God for my good and the good of others. My molestation can be useful. The loss of a child can be useful. He can work it all together so it can be good, useful. It will not only be useful for me, but others, and ultimately for God, as He accomplishes His purposes for our good. Take heart, my friend: all things can be useful!

Although we know God can take all things and work them for good here on earth, we can't forget about the spiritual work He is doing. The ultimate good is being conformed to the image of His son, Jesus.

God has predestined this to take place. This happens through sanctification. I love the way *sanctification* is defined in the Ligonier blog on sanctification. *Sanctification* is . . .

> the work of God's free grace, whereby
> we are renewed in the whole man after

the image of God, and are enabled more and more to die unto sin and live unto righteousness. It is a continuing change worked by God in us, freeing us from sinful habits and forming in us Christ-like affections, dispositions, and virtues. It does not mean that sin is instantly eradicated, but it is also more than a counteraction, in which sin is merely restrained or repressed without being progressively destroyed. Sanctification is a real transformation, not just the appearance of one.[1]

This is what's taking place through our suffering. God does not only use it altogether for an earthly good but, most importantly, a spiritual good. God had gone before us and determined that it would all be used to conform us to the image of His Son. A restoration process is taking place through it all!

That means we might not always see or be able to identify the good that has come from our suffering, or will come from our suffering. Don't misunderstand—you may never get to a point in this life where you say, "I know why this bad thing happened; it produced this other good thing." You will never be able to say that with certainty because you can't read God's mind! But what you can say is, "I know God used this to conform me to the image of His Son, Jesus Christ, and that is the best thing that could happen for me."

So let me sum it up: God uses all of the junk to make us look more like Jesus! What a good God we serve. Talk about what the enemy means for harm and God will use for good! God's ultimate goal is to form us to be more like Jesus, and He will use everything we experience to accomplish this.

"For Those Who Love God"

Who is Paul talking about? If there is a promise to be claimed, we must know whom the promise is for. He says it's for those who love God, who are called for His purpose. The called ones he is speaking about are children of God—Christians. Confidence comes from being a child of God. Children of God can walk in faith that God is sovereign and sees every detail of their lives. Children of God are uniquely cared for by Him.

Not all people can claim this verse, but children of God can.

I have four children. I would say I do a pretty good job of caring for them. I feed them, protect them, and provide for their every need before they ask for it. It's not only my role as their father, but it's my honor. I love being a father.

But this same love and care stops with them. I don't treat the neighbor's children with this type of love and care. I don't even do it for the children at our church. I only do it for my children, and they walk in confidence in this because of who I am and what I have done.

The same is true for God. He only works things together for those who love Him—that is, those who are His children. His children are those who have submitted to the rule and authority of Christ and acknowledge Him as Lord and Savior. When we do that, we are adopted into God's family and can claim this truth. At that moment God begins to restore and redeem the brokenness in our lives. He collects all of the junk and works it all together so it has purpose and meaning.

How can you have confidence that your junk will work together for good? Easy. Do you love Him? *Do you love Him?* Paul says that all things will work for good for those who love Him, for those who are His children.

Artists have always amazed me. They can see things others can't see and express things in such a tangible and meaningful way. One of the types of art that baffles me is junk art. Junk artists typically collect things that have been thrown away or that others don't see any use for.

Some artists even go into landfills looking for what they consider valuable pieces of trash. You may have heard it said, "One man's trash is another man's treasure." Well, this is certainly true for these artists. They see value in pieces of junk. In fact, to them, it's not junk at all; it has value and can be used! After collecting trash and other junk items, they put everything together to make a beautiful piece of art. They take something that was seen as having no value and add value to it by what they do with it. Isn't that amazing? Junk artists have a true gift and eye for this!

But there isn't a better artist than God. He is the greatest junk artist. He takes the junk in our lives, the pieces we've discarded, and makes those things good and valuable. Scripture says we are His masterpiece! He is the artist who takes the broken pieces of our shattered lives and begins to piece them together in a way that only He can, so that it all works together for our good and His glory. Only God can do this!

Questions for Reflection

1. What are some areas in your life that you doubt God can use?

2. Take time to think about how God might use those. Do you believe He can?

3. What junk do you need to hand over to Him so that He can use it?

"Our Junk, His Masterpiece"

CHAPTER 6

Trust

*Assured Reliance on the Character,
Ability, Strength, or Truth of
Someone or Something*

I don't know about you, but I don't trust very easily. I've been betrayed, misled, backstabbed, and deceived, and it's left me a skeptic. The human heart is unpredictable, and it seems like loyalty and trust are lost traits. People have come into my life and assured me they weren't like the others, they wouldn't do those things, but they did. And every single time trust is broken, I look at myself in the mirror and wonder if something is wrong with me that has caused so much of this to take place.

Am I not worthy of a trustworthy relationship? Is something wrong with my character that invites this? I begin not to trust who I am and my ability to keep healthy relationships.

I look at the world through the lens of mistrust.

We live in a world where most things aren't what they appear to be. Social media is filled with people's highlight reels, and most of it isn't real life. People edit and filter their pictures because they don't trust that people will accept them the way they are. We exaggerate stories because we don't trust that the truth is sufficient to keep people around. At the end of the day, it's all built around a lack of trust.

The constant lies, betrayal, and failure to deliver have most of us in a place where we're skeptical of the people we encounter. The art of keeping a secret seems to be lost. People have broken our trust, and we have broken theirs. We've opened ourselves up only to be hurt again. We've trusted only to be disappointed and let down. We've even invested in people only to see them turn against us. Sometimes it feels like we are living in a cycle of mistrust.

There is a phrase we are all familiar with: "innocent until proven guilty." This means one is not considered guilty until the judge has declared them guilty. They are innocent until proven otherwise by substantial evidence. Most of us don't live this way. We live with a "guilty until proven innocent" approach. Our life experiences have taught us not to give away our trust too quickly or to give others the benefit of the doubt. We size people up and give them the third degree before we let them in. We keep them at a distance and only let them into the pieces of our life that won't hurt much if they turn on us. But letting them in all the way and giving them access to hurt us? That takes years of trust building. People have to earn trust.

Some of us have the "mistrust is given and trust earned" motto. Those who function like this typically have a deep suspicion of people and especially those in authority. When someone does something nice that seems too good to be true, we think that there must be a hidden motive behind their actions. No motive appears to be pure, and nothing anyone can do can fast-forward how we trust. It takes time. Failed relationships, parental disappointment, lies, betrayal, and continued failure from those we once trusted have placed most of us in this position. We don't want to live and function this way, but it's how we have learned to survive.

We are in a culture that encourages us to be skeptical of one another, especially those in authority. Recently, a Pew survey noted that Americans trust military, clergy, scientists, and academics less than ever. Additionally, 51 percent of Americans say we cannot trust one another.[1]

When we have a loss of trust in authority, everyone suffers. It is affecting just about every area of our country.

Church attendance is in decline across our nation. Americans are turning away from authority figures and placing themselves first. Why? Because there is great mistrust in our world. People are tired of being hurt and let down so they do whatever they can to guard themselves.

The Edelman Trust Barometer measures the faith people place in leading authorities: government, business, NGOs, and media. It began in 2000 as a way to measure what people think about these institutions in civic life. In 2017, the Trust Barometer registered its decline in all four groups, with more than 50 percent of people believing none of the groups "do what's right."[2] In the most recent report, 57 percent said the government does not work for the good of all people and only 10 percent believe the government is good at what it does.[3] They note that 57 percent of people believe the information they receive is not trustworthy even from news sources, and 66 percent of Americans do not believe leaders can actually address our nation's challenges.[4] The report says that global cynicism is on the rise, and more and more people lose faith in formerly authoritative institutions, citing that none of these four institutions scored more than 50 percent when people were asked if the institution was "ethical or competent." We don't trust authority.

Lee Raine, Scott Peter, and Andrew Perrin write: "Some see fading trust as a sign of cultural sickness and national decline. Some also tie it to what they perceive to be increased loneliness and excessive individualism. About half of Americans (49%) link the decline in interpersonal trust to a belief that people are not as reliable as they used to be."[5] In terms of religion, only 50 percent of adults ages eighteen to twenty-nine trust religious leaders while 71 percent over the age of fifty trust religious leaders, and the thirty to forty-nine demographic finds only 57 percent trust religious leaders.[6]

Did those statistics bring a sobering reality? They did for me. We do not trust as quickly as we did in the past. And our mistrust of authority figures, including religious ones, has turned into a mistrust of God as well. People have a hard time trusting God.

Barna Research Group released its 2015 study and found that one in four Americans don't believe in God, and one of the main reasons is because they have lost trust in the church.[7]

You don't have to look very far to find someone who has lost trust in the church. Whether it's because of a broadscale church scandal or the personal church hurt someone has experienced, many are wounded and angry with God.

I have certainly been there. I don't trust people very quickly, and I don't always trust God. When my father left, trust was broken. When I was molested, trust was broken. When I faced betrayal and my character was assaulted, trust was broken. It left me asking, "Where were You in all of this, God?"

My Mess: If God Is for Us

Romans 8:31 says, "What then shall we say to these things? If God is for us, who can be against us?" What a powerful statement. But what exactly does it mean?

> If God is for us, who can be against us?

To be honest, I don't always trust that passage. I don't always trust that God is for me. I wrestle with it because of internal factors. My finite mind cannot fully comprehend how the Creator of the universe, the one who hung the moon and the stars, is for me. And I don't often trust that I am "fearfully and wonderfully made" (Ps. 139:14) because I sure do feel too messed up to be "fearfully and wonderfully made." I wrestle with this truth.

And I wrestle with this truth because of external factors. My circumstances don't always seem to line up with what these Bible verses say. If God is for me, why didn't He protect me when I was a young boy? If He is for me, then why does it seem like I lose more than I win? If He is for me, then why do I have so many critics who have shattered my confidence? My past experiences created a relationship with God that left me doubting whether He is for me. I haven't always felt protected by Him. I still wear the scars from being misunderstood, criticized, and ridiculed. These experiences cut me deeply. And I felt like God, my Father, didn't step up for me, His son. How does that show He is for me?

Do you ever feel that way? If you peel back the layers of your relationship with God, would you find areas of your life where you don't trust Him? I know it is absurd for me to doubt the Creator of the universe and His love for me after I have so much proof that He is for me, but I do. How can He be for me if so many things in this world seem to be against me?

His Message: "If God Is for Me..."

"What then shall we say to these things? If God is for us, who can be against us?" What are the *things* Paul is talking about?

Up to this point Paul has shared some profound, earth-shattering truths about our freedom from condemnation, our adoption, Christ's atoning death, suffering, creation, and future glory. These are the *things* Paul is speaking of. In light of these things, what shall we say? What should be our response?

He answers this question with a rhetorical question: *"If God is for us, who can be against us?"* It's as if he says, "After all God has done for us, why in the world do you fear anything that could come your way?"

If...

Have you ever wondered if God is truly for you? You may have asked yourself, "If God was for me, then why (fill in the blank)?" Maybe deep pain or delayed blessings have caused you to ask yourself that question. Or seeing people around you prosper more than you are when you have been faithful. I promise you, He is for you, and there is plenty of evidence to back this up!

In Ephesians 2:1–3, we see that the God who is for us *rescued* us. "And you were dead in the trespasses and sins in which you once walked, following the course of this world, following the prince of the power of the air, the spirit that is now at work in the sons of disobedience—among whom we all once lived in the passions of our flesh, carrying out the desires of the body and the mind, and were by nature children of wrath, like the rest of mankind."

Do you know what that means? It means that we were spiritually dead. We were zombies walking around with no spiritual life.

Sometimes we think of Christianity as some sort of additive we put into our lives to make it better. Maybe you're a morning coffee drinker, but you don't like it black—you take it with a little dose of almond milk and sugar. That additive, for you, enhances your coffee. We sometimes think of Christianity that way—we add it to our lives to make things a little bit better.

When we think of Christianity this way, it prevents us from seeing how dire our situation was before Christ. Before you were a Christian, you weren't a perfectly normal cup of coffee in need of a little Jesus additive to make you a bit smoother and sweeter. Nor were you just a little uneducated, in need of a teacher. Nor were you a little spiritually sick, in need of some medicine. Paul says you were *dead*.

Spiritually dead.

You weren't kicking trying to keep your head above the water, in need of a life raft. You were on the ocean floor, with no oxygen in your lungs.

Paul goes on. You weren't only spiritually dead; you were being led by Satan (the prince of the power of the air). This idea can be really offensive to people today. *Okay, sure, I did some messed-up things,* you may be thinking, *but I wasn't being led by the devil!* The Bible disagrees with you. Paul says that all people who are outside of Christ, who haven't been born again, are under the power of Satan.

And we were carrying out the passions of our flesh that led us to be children of wrath. Our desires were distorted. Like a drug addict who can't get enough of the very thing that will kill him, you and I had desires that led us not to life but to more death. Our sinful passions—lust, anger, jealousy, bitterness—were killing us, but we couldn't get enough of them. Therefore, we were under God's just and holy wrath.

We were doomed!

We had a full ride straight to hell, with room and board paid for. And we would have continued on that path if God in His mercy didn't rescue us.

God didn't save us because we had so much to offer Him and He needed our skills and gift set. No—we have absolutely nothing to offer God. He is not impressed or motivated by anything we have. He doesn't need anything from us. It is all motivated by one thing: His love.

The next verses say, "But God, being rich in mercy, because of the great love with which he loved us, even when we were dead in our trespasses, made us alive together with Christ—by grace, you have been saved" (Eph. 2:4–5).

Did you get that? It doesn't say we changed our minds about how we were living and decided to pursue Christ. Dead people can't change their minds! No. It was all done by His grace, not by anything we did.

> We have absolutely nothing to offer God. He is not impressed or motivated by anything we have. He doesn't need anything from us.

If God weren't for us, He would have left us that way, dead, at the bottom of the ocean. But instead, He spared His Son and gave Him up for us all. If God did this, why in the world do we question whether He can be trusted with our other needs? He took care of the greatest need we would ever have so we can walk in confidence that He is for us.

Do you believe this? Has God made you spiritually alive yet? Have you trusted in Jesus' death and resurrection for your sins? If not, what are you waiting for?

He Intercedes for Us

Jesus is interceding for us. Do you realize what this means? It's more than His being a friend or "homeboy," as you might see on some T-shirts. It's much more than that! It means that Jesus, after dying on the cross and defeating death, is now sitting at the right hand of the Father and is working on our behalf.

Did you get that? Jesus is currently working on *your* behalf. He is interceding for *you* and always will be. He won't grow weary or walk out on you. He is going to do it whether you trust Him or not. His intercession for us is not based on our faithfulness; it's based on His! Praise God for that, because we wouldn't have much confidence in His intercession if it were based on our faithfulness.

I am not sure if you have ever had someone who is always watching your back and looking out for you. Someone who truly loves you for you and not for what you do. I have a great friend like this that I have known since college. He isn't jealous or envious. He doesn't compare, accuse, or attack me. This guy continually watches my back, loves me well, rebukes me well, and does it all in love. It is an incredible feeling to have someone like that in my corner.

This is what Christ is like for us. He's in our corner. He doesn't want anything from you and doesn't need you to perform for Him. He just loves you. You mean so much to Him, and He will continue to speak to the Father on your behalf. He has cleared your debt and paid for your future. He is for you!

He Fights for Us

If God is for us, who can be against us? Well, I can give you a long list of people who are against me.

I really can.

Being a pastor doesn't always mean that I hold a popular seat. It means I open myself up to criticism, slander, and attacks on my character. The emails and text messages flood me weekly with things I should be doing better as a pastor. It's never-ending and feels like I can never do enough.

The *who can be against us* doesn't mean we will be the most popular in the room, but it does mean we will be the most covered in the room. Part of Christ interceding on our behalf means He fights for us. Who can condemn or bring any charge? This means God, the greatest fighter and defender, fights for us. He is the undefeated and undisputed champion. He has never lost a fight. No one has ever come close to defeating Him. He TKOs His opponents, and Scripture tells us that this same God is fighting for us.

It's not that we won't have any opponents; it's that we don't need to fear our petty opponents who ultimately have to go through Him to get to us. We can read Paul's rhetorical question as, "Who can be against us and have any shot as success?" No one. So why do we allow them to cause so much havoc and stress in our lives? Their emails, text messages, and passive-aggressive sleights can only go so far.

This passage doesn't mean we won't have any opposition. Quite the contrary. Christians have plenty of resistance. The opposition may come from family, friends, coworkers, or demonic forces. We will have to fight through people being against us for the rest of our lives. But listen to several rhetorical questions Paul asks: "Who will bring any accusation against God's elect? And who will condemn?" (see Rom. 8:33–34). People will accuse and attempt to condemn you, and it will cause you significant pain. It may even feel like it has gained traction. But be encouraged—their accusation and condemnation will not hold up in God's court. It may make some traction in man's court but not in God's.

Feeble people cannot thwart the plans the Creator has for you. Having opposition doesn't mean God isn't for us;

instead, it's the reality of the broken world we live in. It's part of Satan's attack on God's children. When people accuse you, they show remnants of being influenced by the enemy. Accusation and condemnation are characteristics of Satan, not God. *Satan* means "adversary or accuser."[8] His goal is to kill, steal, and destroy (John 10:10). He is our ultimate opponent and has no mercy for his ene-

> Feeble people cannot thwart the plans the Creator has for you.

mies. Satan wants to bring so much pain to the believer's life so that we will turn from God and no longer trust Him or follow Him.

How many times have you heard of people who do not believe in God or are angry with God because of the pain they have experienced in their life? Satan may have caused the pain and suffering they faced; he uses it to turn people away from God. Division and broken relationships have his fingerprints all over them. He condemns and falsely accuses and often influences Christians to do it to one another. When Christians or any other person takes the accuser's position, they are being affected by a spirit of accusation and division. This isn't the heart of God.

Growing up, I was involved in a lot of street fights. Sometimes it was my way of surviving in the neighborhood, and other times it was because my older cousins would set up a match for me just for their entertainment. Other times my fighting came in the form of protecting myself from being molested. And in some cases it was fighting for my emotional stability. I did a lot of defending myself. It was second nature to me. I never had a father to swoop in and come to my rescue, so I learned how to survive for myself. I never really depended on anyone else to fight my battles for me. When opposition attacks, my first instinct is still to put on the boxing gloves and begin defending myself. I'm still learning how to allow God to be my protector.

The Example of David

David was great at this. Some said he was too young and laughed at the thought of him stepping up to the plate to fight Goliath. But he gives us great insight on how to let God fight for us. Let's take a look.

In 1 Samuel 17, David steps into the ring with Goliath. You can almost hear the announcer saying, "Ladies and gentlemen, in this corner from Gath, we have the nine-foot giant, Goliath. In the other corner, coming in at five-foot-nothing, a teenager from the wilderness, David."

The crowd roars and cheers, expecting to see a bloodbath take place. The Israelites aren't even in the crowd. They never came out of the locker room, too embarrassed to see their representative get whipped. They slightly peel back the curtains to see what's about to take place. And when they do, David gives them—and us—three great examples to follow.

David Trusted the Promise of the Covenant

Before the blows take place, it's almost as if David chuckles and yells, "He's uncircumcised, he's uncircumcised" (vv. 26, 36; paraphrased). This would certainly be an awkward taunt in a fight in the twenty-first century. Why was this significant? Why was David saying this?

Circumcision was the sign of God's covenant with Abraham and his offspring, the Israelites. This covenant meant they belonged to God. It showed that you were one of His people and in a position of protection and covering.

David was circumcised; therefore, he was in covenant with God. This gave him the confidence he needed to pursue the battle because he knew God would be with him. David also knew Goliath was not circumcised, which meant he had no covering and wasn't protected. Not only that, but David knew that part of God's covenant with Abraham and his offspring was to bless those who bless them and curse those who treat them with contempt (Gen. 12:3). David knew, because of God's covenant, that God was going to be on his side, against Goliath.

David had confidence in his standing with God, and he moved forward from a position of trust knowing that God was with him. If God was with him, what could this Philistine possibly do against him? If God was with David, who could be against him?

There is excellent news on this front. Today we don't have to be circumcised the way the Jewish males did in David's time; that was the Old Testament covenant. Instead, we received the circumcision of the heart by placing faith in Jesus. If you have done that, then praise God, you are covered and in a covenant with God that you can put your confidence in. How certain is this covenant? Jesus bought it with His blood on the cross. God—who cannot lie or change His mind—will certainly keep that covenant forever!

This means protection, security, and covering! If God is for you, then what "Philistine" can be against you? Trust in the covenant; He is for you!

David Trusted that if God Did It Once, Then God Can Do It Again

David entered this battle being told why he couldn't win: "You are but a youth" (1 Sam. 17:33). Yet he stayed focused, remembering whose he was, not just who he was. If he focused on who he was, he would have focused on his youth, inexperience, and lack of proper military training. Instead he focused on whose he was. He remembered what God had already done for him, and he trusted that God could do it again.

He recalled that God helped him defeat a lion and take a lamb from a bear's mouth. And if God was with him in the battles of the wilderness, then God would be with him in the fight against Goliath.

When we look at our struggles, we can be overcome with worst-case scenarios and paralyzed with hypotheticals. We must pause long enough to remember the times God has come through and fought for us. If He did it once, we can trust that He can do it again! Trust His track record; He is for you!

David Trusted in Who God Is

In 1 Samuel 17:45, David introduces a new name for God: *Jehovah Tsaba*. *Tsaba* is the Hebrew term for "host." It is found 486 times in the Hebrew Bible. It typically refers to some type of military entity like an army. *Tsaba* functions as an attribute of Jehovah. He is over all. He is the source of existence. He is the source of power. Occasionally, the writers of the Hebrew Bible intensify this title with the name Jehovah Elohim Tsaba: Yahweh, the God of Hosts (Armies).

This is the relational-Creator-Ruler name to indicate the personal God is also the Creator God, who is over all rulers, armies, false gods, and other spiritual powers. Do you know what this means? It means that when God, the commander in chief, came on the scene, Goliath didn't stand a chance. David may have thrown the stone, but God who gave him the victory.

So, child of God, take a deep breath. Remember that if you are in a covenant with God, you have Jehovah Tsaba on your side. Introduce your problems to Jehovah Tsaba and let *Him* do the rest. Trust His name; He is for you!

What opposition are you facing right now? If you aren't facing any yet, it will come your way. People will accuse you and attempt to condemn you, but those "Philistines" can't thwart the plans God has for you. You can trust Him.

If you struggle to fully trust Him, guess what? He will still be for you. It's not about the strength of your trust but the strength of the One whom you trust.

If you get mad at Him for allowing opposition to gain traction, guess what? He will always be for you! He's big enough and strong enough to handle our doubts and frustrations.

> When God, the commander in chief, came on the scene, Goliath didn't stand a chance.

It's who He is, and He won't ever stop! He is for you, and you can trust that!

Questions for Reflection

1. Do you have a tough time trusting people? Why?

2. Do you have a tough time trusting God? Why?

3. What aren't you trusting God with?

⌒

"He Will Fight for You"

~~~

CHAPTER 7

Separation Anxiety

Excessive Fear or Worry about Separation from Home or an Attachment Figure

One of my greatest fears is being separated from those I love. Whether through death, divorce, dysfunction, or distance, I fear separation.

Not sure exactly which it is, but as long as I can remember, there has always been a deeply rooted insecurity in my soul about being abandoned.

This fear has never allowed me to make deep and meaningful relationships. The trauma I experienced from abuse and betrayal trained me not to let anyone get close enough to hurt me. Can you relate to this? A façade has been put up so that everything on the outside looks great, but on the inside you are terrified of another failed relationship. On the one hand, you're too scared of abandonment to let yourself get close to anyone, but on the other hand, you're afraid of losing the same people you've kept from getting too close?

My Mess: Loneliness

I am an extreme introvert who comes off as a charismatic, crowd-engaging guy. On the outside, you would think everything in my life is excellent. I have a beautiful wife, four beautiful children, degrees on my wall, and a thriving church. But, when you peel back the layers, you will find a lonely man. A lonely man who is screaming on the inside, "Please don't leave me."

I am a person who is surrounded by hundreds yet not known by many. Deep inside, there is yearning for affirmation, a man who desperately wants to be accepted. I want to know that my imperfections won't cause someone to run and that my perfections won't entice them to stay. I long for a community filled with the character of God, one that doesn't require perfection and performance but instead is founded on grace, mercy, and unconditional love. I want to show people the good, bad, and ugly and not run away when the ugly is too much to handle. I want to be fully known and fully loved, yet I fear that to be fully known would prevent me from being fully loved.

This makes community hard for me. My mind knows God has created me to be in community, but my emotions won't allow for it.

It all compounded over the years, and although my heart longs for community, I have found it safer to settle for loneliness.

After you have walked through life and experienced enough relational dysfunction, it shatters the image you have of yourself. Fear slowly takes root deep within your soul that reminds you of the past hurts and keeps the door to the real you locked. We think if people only knew what we've done, what we've thought, what we've looked at, or how we look on the inside, they would reject us. So instead, we settle for the alternative—to be connected intellectually but separated emotionally.

It's an interesting dichotomy. Then, once we have let someone in, a fear runs through our minds like a rushing river: "Will they use the bad against

> We think if people only knew what we've done, what we've thought, what we've looked at, or how we look on the inside, they would reject us.

me? Will they turn on me? Will they leave me?" Thoughts like this turn us into prisoners of our vulnerability. We gave people a piece of the real us, and now they can reject it and make our fears turn into reality: rejection and separation.

When people open up and are vulnerable to others, an invisible covenant takes place. For the vulnerable, the covenant is that now there is an attachment to this person because they have been given a piece of them that typically isn't given away. When the vulnerable party opens up, they assume the recipient will not go anywhere or ever do anything to hurt them. But as soon as the relationship starts taking a turn for the worst, panic and anxiety set in. It seems like the separation is just around the corner.

I remember my first significant experience with separation anxiety. It came when I was developing a relationship with my wife. We were living in San Francisco. I was attending seminary, and she was a preschool teacher. It was August 2009, and some friends were throwing me a birthday party. At this point in my life, I was in my late twenties and was laser focused on finishing seminary. Although I desired marriage one day, I wasn't looking at that moment and hadn't been on a date in a long time. My wife was new to the area and didn't know many people, so someone invited her to my party. She walked into the room, and her beauty was captivating. From time to time, I glanced over to see how she interacted with people. I wanted to play it cool, so I stayed away from her and kept my distance. She was funny, friendly, and thoughtful. Her love for people and Jesus radiated. She was almost too good to be true—beautiful inside and out!

Guys at the party took notice and surrounded her for the rest of the night. I honestly thought, *Great, one of these knuckleheads is going to win her heart, and she's not even going to notice me.* Part of this thought process was because I was twenty-seven, and in seminary world, that seems *old* for a single dude. It seemed like the marriage train was passing me by. At this point in my life, I had performed ceremonies, been the best man at weddings, and attended more than my fair share, and all of it felt like a big slap in the face. Dating never worked out for me. I had short stents, but it just never went anywhere.

It's going to sound crazy and vain, but I didn't have much money, I didn't own a home, and my car was a beater. Oh, and did I mention I was also going bald. So I was every woman's dream guy. Not really.

I wasn't a very desirable man, had a jacked-up past, wasn't a virgin, and had a history filled with drugs and alcohol. I wasn't your average seminary student. Because of this, I thought I was too stained to be loved by anyone.

I'll fast-forward to spare the awkward details of my pursuit, but several months later my wife and I were dating. It was no doubt from God. We were on cloud nine, and we were a match made in heaven. I was falling hard for her. It was perfect, and it scared me.

I wanted to end it all.

I tried to break it off. All of a sudden, it hit me: *she can hurt me.* I had divulged all this information about myself and peeled back the layers of my soul. She knew all my junk and had the power to crush me. I started panicking, thinking about the possibility of her leaving me. Separation anxiety kicked in. I couldn't sleep. I couldn't eat. I was terrified to lose her. I was scared. I didn't trust that she would stay. I let her see every part of my shattered soul, and she had the power to reject it all.

When she went home to visit family, I feared that she would come back and decide I wasn't the man she wanted. When she hung out with friends, I feared her meeting someone better and leaving me. The vicious cycle went on and on.

I didn't want to lose her. I deeply feared being rejected and alone.

Let me define what this means practically. Separation anxiety can be debilitating. It's when you excessively fear being detached from the person who gives you security, comfort, and love. It keeps you from making healthy relationships and leaves you feeling isolated and lonely.

If you have kids, you probably know a little about separation anxiety. When little boys and girls start to become more aware of their moms and dads, who give them safety and security and comfort, they can become really scared of being away from those sources of security. So, when it's time to drop them off at school, or have a babysitter come over, a child can become anxious. This is normal, and most kids outgrow it pretty quickly. But having separation anxiety as an adult can be much more debilitating.

It overtakes a person's perception of reality. The emotions experienced become unpredictable and unrealistic. The fear consumes and haunts an individual, and any sign of separation from someone they love puts them into a deep panic. When the relationship seems strained or on its last leg, the fear leads them to overcompensate, hoping it will cause the one they love not to go anywhere. It's exhausting and relationally paralyzing. This is what happened to me in just about every significant relationship I had. The anxiety would enter, and the cycle of fear and abandonment would flood my emotions. I feared being all alone. Where does this come from?

He Never Came

My father gave the appearance of being a "man's man." He was strong, macho, and carried himself with extreme confidence. I remember him as a scruffy-faced man who smoked Marlboro cigarettes, drank Miller Lite, and had greasy hands from working on cars. He was short-tempered and abusive to my mother. Our nights were filled with yelling, abuse, and alcohol.

After many nights of this, my mother finally took a stand and separated from my father. The separation meant that we would live apart from my father but he would pick us up on the weekends for visitation. But he never came. Friday after Friday my mother would drop us off at our grandmother's place so that my father could pick us up, but he never came. Weeks turned into months, and months turned into years. I waited as long as I could. My brother became weary of waiting, and he knew my father wasn't coming. I held on a little longer and would watch for his red van from the patio. But he never came. This destroyed me. I wondered if I wasn't worthy enough of his love. I questioned if I had done something wrong. It was incomprehensible to me as to why a father would not come get his child. This planted a separation anxiety in me that would never go away.

Lonely but Not Alone

Have you ever dealt with separation anxiety? Do you settle now for being lonely rather than experiencing the pain of being separated again? As a culture we are more connected than ever yet more lonely than we've ever been. But there is something that most of us have in common: the fear of rejection, separation, and loneliness.

Studies show that kids grow up now more connected than ever, yet they are coined the Lonely Generation. The Health Resources & Services Administration has an entire website called "The Loneliness Epidemic."[1]

A 2018 survey by *The Economist* and the Kaiser Family Foundation shows that 22 percent of American adults "always feel lonely," and 46 percent of Americans "always or sometimes feel alone." Fifty-four percent of Americans say they always or sometimes feel that no one knows them well. Loneliness is linked to depression, anxiety, and delirium and is the number one fear of millennials.[2]

But how is that? There are so many social platforms that allow us to be connected: Facebook (2.38 billion users), Twitter (369 million users), Snapchat (189 million daily users), and Instagram (500 million daily users).[3] On the surface, we aren't alone at all. Gamers are connected to others and participate in an online community with people they don't know. Yet when the power turns off, the loneliness sets back in, and the craving to jump back online to avoid the empty feeling returns.

How can we be connected to millions of people in millions of different ways yet feel unseen, unknown, and lonely? We want to be known and loved, but we are too afraid to let people in, so we settle for loneliness instead.

Nobody wants to be alone. People may want to be left alone, but they don't want to be alone.

Have you ever walked into a coffee shop and seen people studying with headphones on? They give the impression that they are focused and don't want to be bothered, but at the same time they don't want to be alone. If they wanted to be alone, they would have stayed home. But instead, they would rather be surrounded by people in a coffee shop with no intention of ever building any relationships. It's become their community. The barista may know their name and drink order. They may see the occasional regulars they nod their head to when they walk in, and all of that seems to be good enough.

> How can we be connected to millions of people in millions of different ways yet feel unseen, unknown, and lonely?

It's a shallow excuse for a community, but it's a safe community that can't hurt them.

In 2005 the singer and rapper Akon released his single "Lonely," and it became a worldwide hit. It reached number two on the charts in several countries and number four in the United States. In this song he sings about how lonely he is; he even calls himself "Mr. Lonely." And this song was a hit!

In October 2020, Justin Bieber released his single by the same title, and it shot up on the music charts, quickly becoming number one in several countries. Bieber expounds on his deep pain of mistakes, rejection, and transparency that caused him to feel alone while surrounded by literally millions of fans.

Why were these songs such hits? Well, you guessed it—because we can all relate. People fear being abandoned and left alone. They fear being separated from others when those others find out who they truly are.

Loneliness in the Psalms

Throughout the Psalms there is a reoccurring theme of being abandoned and forgotten by God. The deep sense of loneliness is one we can all relate to. The experiences of the psalmists became married to their emotions in a way that divorced God from the present pains in their lives.

This is the organic response to the sense of God's being absent. It's a torturous feeling to think that God has left. Being separated from God may be our greatest fear. The psalmist has experienced something earth-shattering in his life that has made him feel as if God has left him. The sense of being separated from His presence has put the psalmist in a place of great despair.

Psalm 42 opens with a sense of longing. The psalmist longs to be with God, who brings refreshment to his soul. There is a deep sense that God has left him.

The writer is thirsty, and that thirst is compared to that of a parched animal. In fact, archeologists have found engraved seals from the seventh and eighth centuries BC that depict a doe wandering in the wilderness seeking water, demonstrating the power this opening phrase had in Jewish culture.[4]

The idea that the soul pants after God demonstrates our utter dependence on Him for life, but even more significantly, it indicates that God is the foundation and source of joy and pleasure.[5] There is a desire to be in the presence of God, in the arms of our loving Father. When we can feel His presence, the despairs of this life do not seem to be as prominent, but once that power of His presence is removed, our experiences no longer make sense.

The soul that thirsts after the living God is thirsting for life.[6] In the climate of the psalmist, streams that still flowed during the dry seasons were called "living waters," and this metaphor points us to God, the Source of life. The writer is lamenting the loss of God's presence

> God is the foundation and source of joy and pleasure.

in corporate worship, and without this presence he feels parched and exhausted. He is the deer panting and looking for living water.

It is unclear why the psalmist cannot meet for corporate worship. He is "prevented and remains distant," and in the midst of that, the enemy taunts. The question, "Where is your God?" (v. 3) might mean that he is outside the land of Israel. There is a sense of exile and longing to approach God in the "festal rituals as before." The festal processions were elaborate and included priests and stringed instruments, singers, and other musicians, who made their way to the temple's entrance in Jerusalem.[7] People followed with branches in hand and danced to the horns of the altar.[8]

The psalmist remembers these processions. The role of memory is influential. The psalmist remembers the divine presence he felt in worship, and without it his soul is starving for the only thing that can fill it. Nothing else can substitute. His soul is tortured, and the reality of this pain is revealing. The psalmist uses a resounding phrase: "Why, my soul, are you so sad? Why are you in such turmoil?" (v. 5). Then he moves to verse 6, where he states he is deeply depressed. Can you see it? Can you feel it? It's tangible! There is a sense that he has been separated from God. It's put his soul in great distress and turmoil. He is hungry to be known and seen by the one true and living God!

There is a hunger pain that reminds us of our yearning to no longer be separated from God. As soon as we are born into this world, our soul begins to hunger. It's as if it knows what it wants and what it needs to make it filled, complete, and whole again, and that is to be reunited with the Father.

This is a reunion that can only take place by placing one's faith in Jesus. Without this love we are left feeling like the psalmist. We are insecure, miserable, and feel abandoned. But praise God, our feelings don't always tell the truth.

I have been at the place in my life where a multitude of friends surrounded me, but I wasn't walking closely with God, and I was lonely. Then I have been at the place where no friends surrounded me, but I was walking so close to God I felt filled. There is something about knowing He is near that fills the empty places of our souls.

Dealing with Separation Anxiety

I slowly but surely learned how to deal with my anxiety and start the path toward healthy relationships. There are several things I have to continually do to defeat the fear that knocks at the door when new relationships begin.

Lower My Expectations of People

My typical approach to relationships would be to mentally place people on a trial run to see how long they could go before they failed to meet my expectations. These expectations were usually unspoken. They consisted of loyalty, commitment, and trust. I looked for signs in the relationships that indicated future betrayal and mistrust. When I felt like anyone broke any of these expectations, I would begin to close off the relationship. I was unintentionally making people prove themselves and pay for my past relational wounds.

As I matured in my walk with Christ, I came to a surprisingly relieving realization: *people will hurt me, and I will hurt people.*

We are imperfect beings who all come with some baggage attached to us. This baggage can come in many forms: insecurities, anxieties, depression, past hurts, etc. When we enter relationships, we not only bring baggage but also attach unrealistic expectations. Sometimes these expectations are assumed and unspoken. When people fail to meet them and fail to be who we think we need them to be for us, then we feel as if we have been betrayed, lied to, and cheated. But let me remind you of something: there is no perfect relationship, and everyone who enters your life has the potential to hurt you intentionally and unintentionally. So lower your expectations of people in your life and learn how to enter relationships with grace.

> There is no perfect relationship, and everyone who enters your life has the potential to intentionally and unintentionally hurt you.

Don't Substitute God

No one in your life can replace God. Not your mother, father, friend, children, or spouse. God has created us to be in a relationship with Him, and He will never allow anything to replace what only He can fill. The late French philosopher Blaise Pascal said, "There is a God-shaped vacuum in the heart of each man which cannot be satisfied by any created thing but only by God the Creator, made known through Jesus Christ."[9]

Did you get that? There is something in us that cannot be satisfied by anything but God alone. We must grasp that truth. Community is needed, even essential, but it is never meant to substitute for relational intimacy with the Creator. I do not mean that I am not careful with who I allow to come into my life, but I do mean I have learned that no one can substitute what only Christ can do for me. It's not my wife's role or anyone else's role to fill the insecurities in my life due to my past. They can never do it, and I will always be let down if I try to make them.

> There is something in us that cannot be satisfied by anything but God alone.

We cannot view people as the solution or compensation for our past wounds. It's not right, fair, or biblical.

His Message: Take God at His Word

The key to walking through separation anxiety and rejection is taking God at His Word. If He said it, then you can rest your life on it.

Romans 8:35 is first seen within the context of whom Paul was writing to, but the nature and character of God found in this text remains faithful to us today: "Who shall separate us from the love of Christ?"

Paul gives us a promise we can count on. He doesn't dispute his readers' feelings, but he helps calm what's probably their greatest fear: being separated from God and left alone in this broken world.

At this point Paul has entered a series of rhetorical "who" questions: "Who shall bring any charge . . . ?" "Who is to condemn?" and the greatest and last question, "Who shall separate us from the love of Christ?"

The answer to the question Paul poses is simple: no one.

We must take time to understand the depth of what Paul is telling the believers of this time. The word Paul uses for separate is *chorizo*; it means "to depart, separate from, or divorce."[10] He asks them this rhetorical question after going through a dissertation of God's defense of and love for His children. The freedom of this truth had to be overwhelming for the listeners. They had just heard how they can no longer be condemned, how they "have received the Spirit of adoption" (v. 15), and how future glory is waiting for them.

He proceeds to give them a list of things so that whatever insecurity they have can be debunked. Paul takes away any excuses we have for not resting in God's love. "For I am sure that neither death nor life, nor angels nor rulers, nor things present nor things to come, nor powers, nor height nor depth, nor anything else in all creation, will be able to separate us from the love of God in Christ Jesus our Lord" (vv. 38–39).

Did you get that list? You can add whatever you want to it and be confident that nothing, absolutely nothing, can separate you from His love.

No addiction, affair, divorce, or mistake can separate you! I am not saying those things don't have consequences, but I am saying, nothing you have done, are doing, or will do, and nothing that has been or will be done to you can separate you from God's love. Come on, somebody! You should take a praise break and praise His name for this truth!

People may have walked out on you, betrayed you, and left you feeling abandoned. But you have a Father who will never leave you or forsake you. He won't run when you mess up. Your sin is not too great for Him. Your mistakes are not going to cause Him to unfriend you or give you the cold shoulder until He gets over it. He's not going to give you the silent treatment and throw a tantrum. That's not who He is!

When we are in Christ, nothing can separate us from His love!

Questions for Reflection

1. Do you feel like you have a healthy view of relationships? Why or why not?

2. What are some ways you have placed unrealistic expectations on people?

3. What are some areas where you have been trying to replace God with created things to satisfy you?

"Lonely but Not Alone"

CHAPTER 8

~⌒

Conquer

To Gain a Surpassing Victory

I don't know about you, but I love a good victorious story. Movies like *Rudy* and *Glory Road* charge me up. These movies depict an underdog who has to fight hard, dig deep, and overcome. The road to victory isn't easy.

In both of these movies, the path to victory is filled with pain, disappointment, and opposition. There are obstacles that seem impossible to overcome, but the underdog seems to defy the odds! That's what makes these movies so good. By the end of the movie, you find yourself angry at the opposition and cheering for Rudy to make the team and the Texas Western Miners to obliterate everyone they face. Victory is much sweeter when it's not just handed to you! But there is no better victory story than the story God writes.

The stories of victory God has written in Scripture are filled with underdogs like Moses, Joshua, Esther, David, and Isaiah. Characters who really can't do it on their own. They don't have enough resources or manpower to accomplish the task ahead, but by the end they persevere, overcome, and pull out a victory!

And guess what . . . the God who helped them overcome and wrote their victory story is the same God who is still writing stories today. And He wants to write yours!

My Mess: My Conqueror Story

By the age of sixteen, I had lost total control of my life. Drugs, sex, and alcohol controlled me, and my hopeless soul had no anchor for hope. Culture and community dictated who I was and what I did.

Truthfully, I didn't care whether I lived or died. I knew I would only live once, and I embraced that to the fullest. I was adventurous, had no fear, and only had one gear in life—full speed. Everything I did, I did it all-in.

I will never forget a teacher pulling me aside and telling me she was afraid for my life. She proceeded to tell me that she had noticed that I was spinning out of control and I tended to go all-in. She was concerned for me. And she was right. I had no regard for my life. I was defeated and felt like the battle was already lost. My grades were bad. I never tried to succeed because I was too afraid to fail. The abuse I faced stole any ounce of confidence I had, and my poor life choices had already been made and couldn't be undone. I felt like a loser who was never going to succeed or accomplish anything, so I embraced the bad-boy image. I figured if I wasn't going to be known for my success and accomplishments, I would be known for being a fun, wild guy. At least being seen as a loser gave me an identity. I embraced being the underdog in all I did.

One night I was on my way home from a wild weekend. My friend was giving me a ride home, and my house was down a three-mile country road with a lot of twists and turns. As we approached a sharp turn, we noticed a vehicle that was smashed against the tree. The hood was consumed in flames that were intensifying. As we approached the vehicle, we noticed there was someone in the car. His head was covered in blood, leaning over the steering wheel. He was unconscious.

The intensity of the fire picked up quickly, engulfing the rest of the vehicle. We pulled over, and my friend called 911. I couldn't help myself. Something in me wouldn't let me sit still and watch. Calling 911 and waiting until they arrived didn't seem sufficient in my sixteen-year-old mind. Another gear kicked in, and I quickly unbuckled my seat belt. My friend panicked and tried to stop me, but I ran to the burning vehicle and tried to open the car door. It was jammed.

At this point every second was crucial because the flames weren't slowing down. The heat consumed me, and the hot steel burned against my arms. I reached in the driver's window and pulled the gentlemen out through the window, dragging him to a safe and secure area. Not long after, the car was engulfed in flames.

The first responders said if we hadn't arrived at the time we did, the gentlemen could have lost his life. That night was exhilarating for me. I loved the challenge, the risk, the adrenaline that came with it all. I saw a situation that seemed like a challenge, and I took it on. It felt like a sweet victory.

Little did I know, this would be part of the story God was writing for my life.

This conquering mentality has never left me. I have seen God mold in me an internal strength that gears up when challenges arise. I want to defeat and conquer tough situations. Losing never seems to be an option for me. When challenges knock on my door, I answer with a mind and strength that comes from dependence on the Lord. I am a fierce competitor who takes anything and everything as a challenge.

This personality isn't always so great when the competitiveness kicks in over a game of Monopoly during Thanksgiving when the in-laws are in town. Or when I am playing in a fundraiser basketball game for our youth ministry. I typically end up making myself look ridiculous. I can't help it. I don't want to lose. I want to obliterate my opponent. I have been this way since I was a child. Growing up the short, skinny kid on the block not only gave me a chip on my shoulder but also instilled in me an underdog mentality. My father was an amateur boxer and a competitor so I am sure this instinct was also inherited.

But it is great when it's ministry focused. When I feel like the enemy is attacking, I tend to buckle down and move forward, leading even stronger in the knowledge that the enemy cannot overcome our God. I thrive in tough situations. I want God to show up like He did with David against Goliath, to dominate the situation and show everyone that He is in charge, and He is my God. I want Him to show up in such a way that it leaves no one wondering if that was God! It's the Shadrach, Meshach, and Abendego type of scenarios. In the fiery furnace in an impossible situation, God shows up and shows everyone that He is the one true and powerful God. I yearn for God to write my story and speak on my behalf!

Who Is Writing Your Victory Story?

As I said before, God writes the best stories. This is why movie producers have taken so many biblical narratives and turned them into movies. Why? Because God writes the best stories. Not us but God. We get ourselves into trouble when we attempt to take the pen out of the author's hand and write our own victory story. It typically doesn't end well and isn't as well written. In fact, it often leaves God cleaning up our mess and making edits to the life errors we've made. But thankfully, He's a patient author, and He doesn't ditch us and find a new character to use. We find this to be true in the life of Moses.

Moses had been the underdog since his birth. He was born into a tough situation. All the odds were stacked against him. He was born during a time of great oppression and an attempt at ethnic cleansing, when all Hebrew male babies had a death sentence placed on them. His mother hid him for three months. What a way to start your life!

Born into a world of hostility, a death sentence was placed on him as an infant, and it doesn't stop there. When his mother could no longer hide him, she made a makeshift basket, placed him in it, and sent it up the river. Are you kidding me? What a horrible start to life.

How traumatic this must have been. What did Moses do to deserve this kind of start in life? It just seems unfair.

But God wasn't done writing. Pharaoh's daughter found Moses, took him in, and raised him in Pharaoh's kingdom. He went from being born poor to living in a palace. Not bad for a guy who had a bad start. He had all he wanted in Pharaoh's kingdom! But the story doesn't end there.

Moses never forgot his roots. He had great compassion for the Hebrew people. Scripture tells us that he saw an Egyptian beating a Hebrew so he "looked this way and that, and seeing no one, he struck down the Egyptian and hid him in the sand" (Exod. 2:12). This has all of the characteristics of a premeditated murder plot. He looked around, struck him down, then hid him. Someone doesn't look around and hide a body unless they know what they are doing is wrong. He was wrong. You almost want to give him a pass for this. Like, let's give the guy a break, he's had a tough life. He saw one of his people getting mistreated!

Why did Moses do this? He lived his entire life overcoming his horrible start, and the story was turning out great! Why did Moses ruin it? Why did he choose to make this horrible mistake at the age of forty and have everything come crumbling down? It was like he just couldn't take it anymore and had a moment when his flesh took over. In that moment he tried to become the author of his own life. That wasn't a God-written moment but a Moses-written moment. And how did it end up? Not well—not well at all. Scripture tells us that "he supposed that his brothers would understand that God was giving them salvation by his hand, but they did not understand" (Acts 7:25).

What was his mistake? He *supposed*. He assumed it to be the case. He thought it was the right thing. He did what was right in his own eyes; his flesh took over and began to write. Not a good idea.

A life of error became a life of terror. Pharaoh ended up calling on all bounty hunters to search and kill Moses. One moment of doing what he thought was right in his own eyes would soon cost him greatly. He hit the road as a fugitive. He left everything and everyone behind and hit the lonely road to nowhere.

> Nothing good ever comes out of trying to write a story we were never intended to write.

Nothing good ever comes out of trying to write a story we were never intended to write. We are the characters, not the authors. But praise God, He is not only the author; He is also the great editor. And He was about to edit Moses' life.

Exodus 2 was a complete mess. A murder, a cover-up, and a fugitive on the run. But the story doesn't end there. God wasn't done writing. If you have a had a bad start or have become the author of your own life and you find yourself in a mess, buckle, up because we are about to see God do what He does best—edit our errors.

Chapter 3 takes a dramatic turn. God calls a fugitive on the run to accomplish a holy task, to deliver the people out of Egypt.

> "I have surely seen the affliction of my people who are in Egypt and have heard their cry because of their taskmasters. I know their sufferings, and I have come down to deliver them out of the hand of the Egyptians and to bring them up out of that land to a good and broad land, a land flowing with milk and honey, to the place of the Canaanites, the Hittites, the Amorites, the Perizzites, the Hivites, and the Jebusites. And now, behold, the cry of the people of Israel has come to me, and I have also seen the oppression with which

the Egyptians oppress them. Come, I will send you to Pharaoh that you may bring my people, the children of Israel, out of Egypt." (vv. 7–10)

If I were Moses, I would have probably been like, "Uh, are you talking to *me*? You have the wrong guy. Do you know what I have done? I'm a murderer. Not to mention I have a lot of other issues in my life. I'm not your guy. I have ruined it all, and there is no hope for me." I would have been flabbergasted at the fact that God would want to use someone like me.

But this was an invitation. An invitation to give God the pen back and allow Him to write the rest of the story for Moses. See, here's the thing. God sees what He can do with us despite our mistakes. He knows how to use feeble people to accomplish a great task. But that can be hard for us to comprehend. We know ourselves too well. We know our failures, our shortcomings, and what we can do. This is probably why Moses responds the way he does. He knows he's a murderer on the run with a bunch of inadequacies. He knows he has issues. He understands that the task before him cannot be done by him. He would need a supernatural work to happen.

Moses gives excuse after excuse: "Who am I?," "What shall I say?," "They won't believe me." And then his famous and last excuse, "But I am slow of speech and of tongue" (Exod. 4:10). He looked at what he had to offer, measured it up to God's task, and saw that it didn't add up.

News flash—it never adds up, and it never will.

God makes space for the supernatural to happen. He intentionally leaves a gap between our giftings and His calling, so that when it is accomplished, all will know that He is God. This is what he tells them: "And I will get glory over Pharaoh and all his host, and the Egyptians shall know that I am the LORD" (Exod. 14:4). He sets up situations in our lives that we can't accomplish so that we will know, and all others will know, that He is Lord of all.

Do you have a gap between your gifting and His call on your life? Great! He is making space for a supernatural work to be done.

Moses gave excuses, but none of them worked. God doesn't need a perfect person to do a perfect work.

After Moses realized that his excuses weren't sufficient, he finally surrendered and trusted God to do the rest. He met obstacle after obstacle and saw God's supernatural power come through in a way where all knew that He is God. God used Moses as a great leader of people to see a supernatural work so all would know that God was with the underdog. Water came out of a rock, manna fell from the sky, pilgrims defeated nations, and an enslaved people were brought into freedom. Oh, and I forgot one more thing—God brought them out by parting the Red Sea! That's a huge deal!

Let's take a look at the text to be reminded of just how big of a deal this is. "So he made ready his chariot and took his army with him, and took six hundred chosen chariots and all the other chariots of Egypt with officers over all of them. And the LORD hardened the heart of Pharaoh king of Egypt, and he pursued the people of Israel while the people of Israel were going out defiantly. The Egyptians pursued them, all Pharaoh's horses and chariots and his horsemen and his army, and overtook them encamped at the sea" (Exod. 14:6–9).

The Israelites are on the run from Pharaoh. They don't have many resources, not much to eat, no weapons to defend themselves, nothing. Absolutely nothing. All they have is sheer terror.

And rightfully so. Pharaoh had the best of the best. His army was well trained, well equipped, and eager to kill. Six hundred chariots, officers, horsemen, and an army were all ready to kill. Can you imagine that? It would be like having hundreds of special forces being unleashed to take out you and your family! You wouldn't stand a chance against them.

And how did the Israelites respond when they saw Pharaoh's special forces in their rearview mirror? Just like any of us would have. "When Pharaoh drew near, the people of Israel lifted up their eyes, and behold, the Egyptians were marching after them, and they *feared greatly*. And the people of Israel *cried out* to the LORD. They said to Moses, 'Is it because there are no graves in Egypt that you have taken us away to die in the wilderness? What have you done to us in bringing us out of Egypt? Is not this what we said to you in Egypt: "Leave us alone that we may serve the Egyptians"? For it would have been better for us to serve the Egyptians than to die in the wilderness'" (Exod. 14:10–12, emphasis added).

They *feared greatly, cried out,* and wished Moses had just left them alone and let them *die* in the wilderness.

They were scared, discouraged, and considered themselves dead meat. Hundreds of men coming after them, running in sheer terror, and the worst-case scenario happens. They are trapped. They come to the Red Sea, and their backs are against the wall. Nowhere to run and nowhere to hide. They come to a moment that would take the power of God, a miracle.

Moses in front of all the Israelites puts his staff down, and the Red Sea is parted. What a moment! A moment of surpassing victory. A moment that showed everyone that God is Moses' God.

It doesn't get any better than that. God is the best author and editor! And He writes the best victory stories. This is the kind of conquering that gets me pumped up! God doesn't use Moses' edits against him; instead, He repurposes them. Moses was victorious in how he led. Why? Because he allowed God to be the author and write the story!

Do you realize that this is the same for us? As a Christian, you can take all of your training, failures, and successes and walk in confidence that you are more than a conqueror because of the work of Christ on the cross. You can have a confidence no one can ever take away because of the one true God we serve. God is our God! And He is still handing out victories.

This is exactly what Paul is trying to convey to the believers in Romans 8. We can have an extreme confidence because the battle is already won. Because of the cross of Christ, we have a surpassing victory that makes us say in confidence that we are more than conquerors!

His Message: More Than Conquerors?

"No, in all these things we are more than conquerors" (Rom. 8:37). A powerful statement. But what exactly does it mean?

We have seen this verse on coffee mugs, bumper stickers, and refrigerator magnets. Others have claimed it as the verse they hold onto when life is hard, a verse that has become an anchor to their soul. In the context of Romans 8, Paul is answering this segment of "who" questions? He is confident that absolutely nothing will be able to separate us from the love of God and that we are more than conquerors.

The Battle Is Won

Paul is describing a battle in this text. It comes at us with a vengeance. There is a strong force that we feel like we cannot overcome. Opposition and brokenness and sin in the world are real, and they have a way of finding us. Paul is responding to a series of "who" questions and then begins the list of opponents that seem to threaten our separation from God: "Shall tribulation, or distress, or persecution, or famine, or nakedness, or danger, or sword?" (v. 35).

No! Absolutely nothing can separate us. He not only says no but then proceeds to let those in Christ know that these things have not only lost their power but that we are more than conquerors. This doesn't mean these opponents that threaten our separation don't have the power and ability to touch us. Instead it means they have lost the ultimate ability to separate us from God. It's like what Paul said in Philippians 1:21: "To live is Christ, and to die is gain." The worst these things can do is take our flesh, but they can never take our soul.

Think of it this way: the One who is fighting for you is much greater than the ones who fight against you.

But just in case that list wasn't enough, Paul expands on it. In verses 38–39, he continues the list with "neither death nor life, nor angels nor rulers, nor things present nor things to come, nor powers, nor height nor depth, nor anything else in all creation."

What a list! Read it again if you have to. There is absolutely nothing that has the power to separate us from God's love, and we are more than conquerors against every opposition we face. This word means that we have a surpassing victory. It means that the list of things Paul mentions not only is defeated, but because of the cross, those things have been *obliterated*. A surpassing victory means that it wasn't even a close game. Your opposition doesn't stand a chance. No matter what it is, it cannot defeat you. As Christians, we can fight *from* victory, not *for* victory, since God has already won our battles.

Thoughts of negativity run wild every day. My past still haunts me, and the battle is still going on. I certainly feel the weight and pain of my past. But there is a truth I must remind myself of, and it's the same one Paul gives his audience. I am more than a conqueror, and that is something no one can ever take away from me.

I have seen how God has repurposed much of what the enemy has intended for harm in my life. I have also seen how the wounds of the enemy will be with me for the rest of my life on earth. That is the tragic effect of sin. Our scars don't just disappear because we are Christians, but instead we look to a greater hope. Our faith allows us to walk forward in confidence because of what Christ has done on the cross.

Scoreboard!

Basketball has always been my passion. I love playing pickup games, and it has always been a huge stress reliever for me. I played in high school, and it kept me out of trouble during the season and allowed me to focus my attention on something productive. Entering my senior year, I made a vow to my coach that I would be a better leader, not get into fights, and work hard. The year prior I was kicked off the team for multiple fights. I was determined to have a better season.

I was a guy who was scrappy and loved to talk a little bit of trash to my opponents. Well, let me be a little more honest. I talked trash to the opponents, team, bench, *and* fans. I loved it. It made for a good challenge. I liked not being liked because it made me feel like the underdog, and it gave me the motivation I needed to win and prove them wrong.

One particular game I remember. I played my heart out. By the fourth quarter we were winning by fifty points. The game was done and the victory was already set. As we looked to cruise into a victory with ease, one of their players started to tell me how horrible and overrated I was. The trash talk became a little more personal, and it had me irritated and wanting to retaliate in a way that I would have the year before. I couldn't believe the guy had the boldness to talk trash when he was losing by fifty points. I wondered if he just didn't see the scoreboard or if he was just plain crazy. I became incredibly irritated, and apparently it was noticeable because my coach yelled at me from the sidelines: "Noe, relax, look at the scoreboard!"

He was right. What was I so angry and frustrated about? This opponent couldn't change the score. All he could do was irritate me on the way to victory. For the rest of the game, all I would say to him when he taunted me was "scoreboard." Every single word that came out of his mouth was met with my response of "scoreboard."

Brothers and sisters in Christ, let me remind you of something. We have an opponent who will taunt you, remind you of the past, and come after you over and over again. You may even feel the pain of the taunts and the things on the list that Paul gives. But remember, all he can do is taunt us on our way to victory. He cannot take away the victory. So the next time the enemy taunts you, remind him of the scoreboard. The score is already set by a surpassing margin. We win! Give God the pen of your life, and let Him write the greatest victory story.

> The next time the enemy taunts you, remind him of the scoreboard.

Questions for Reflection

1. What does "more than a conquer" mean in your life?

2 How can you live this truth out?

3 Who is writing your story, you or God?

~~~~~~

"Who's Writing Your Story?"

Notes

Chapter 1: Shame

1. David Guzik, "Genesis 2—Creation Completed; Adam in the Garden of Eden, *Enduring Word*, accessed June 11, 2021, https://enduringword.com/bible-commentary/genesis-2.

2. "Psalm 32:4," *Bible Study Tools*, accessed June 11, 2021, https://www.biblestudytools.com/commentaries/treasury-of-david/psalms-32-4.html.

Chapter 2: Battle

1. "Mind Matters: How to Effortlessly Have More Positive Thoughts," *TLEX Institute*, accessed June 11, 2021, https://tlexinstitute.com/how-to-effortlessly-have-more-positive-thoughts.

2. National Network of Depression Centers 2019 statistics, accessed June 11, 2021, https://nndc.org/facts/?gclid=EAIaIQobChMI9YqI84uT5wIVvf7jBx0gqw5OEAAYASAAEgLv4PD_BwE.

3. Kevin Bonsor, "How Landmines Work," *How Stuff Works*, accessed June 11, 2021, https://science.howstuffworks.com/land-mine.htm.

4. Most often attributed to Lao Tzu, an ancient Chinese philosopher.

Chapter 3: Philophobia

1. "Adoption Statistics," *Adoption Network*, accessed June 11, 2021, https://adoptionnetwork.com/adoption-myths-facts /domestic-us-statistics.

Chapter 4: Suffering

1. C. S. Lewis, *A Grief Observed* (New York: HarperCollins, 2001), 6.
2. John Piper, "Why I Abominate the Prosperity Gospel," *Desiring God*, accessed June 12, 2021, https://www.desiringgod. org/interviews/why-i-abominate-the-prosperity-gospel--2.

Chapter 5: Purpose

1. Nathan W. Bingham, "What Is Sanctification?," *Ligonier Ministries,* June 24, 2013, accessed June 12, 2021, https://www. ligonier.org/blog/what-sanctification.

Chapter 6: Trust

1. Lee Raine, Scott Peeter, and Andrew Perrin, "Trust and Distrust in America," July 22, 2019, https://www.people-press .org/2019/07/22/trust-and-distrust-in-america.
2. Matthew Harrington, "Survey: People's Trust Has Declined in Business, Media, Government, and NGOs," *Harvard Business Review,* January 16, 2017, accessed June 12, 2021, https://hbr.org/2017/01/survey-peoples-trust-has -declined-in-business-media-government-and-ngos.
3. "Edelman Trust Barometer 2020," *Edelman*, accessed June 12, 2021, https://www.edelman.com/sites/g/files/aatuss 191/files/2020-01/2020%20Edelman%20Trust%20Barometer %20Global%20Report.pdf.
4. Ibid., 17.

5. Raine, Peeter, and Perrin, "Trust and Distrust in America."

6. Ibid.

7. Stoyan Zaimov, "1 in 4 Americans Don't Believe in God; Lack of Trust in Local Churches Cited as a Reason Why Adults Are Leaving the Faith," *The Christian Post*, March 25, 2015, accessed June 12, 2012, https://www.christianpost.com /news/barnas-2015-state-of-atheism-report-finds-one-in-four -americans-dont-believe-god-exists.html.

8. "Satan," *Bible Study Tools,* accessed June 12, 2021, https:// www.biblestudytools.com/dictionary/satan.

Chapter 7: Separation Anxiety

1. https://www.hrsa.gov/enews/past-issues/2019/january-17/ loneliness-epidemic

2. Neil Howe, "Millennials and the Loneliness Epidemic," *Forbes*, May 3, 2019.

3. These numbers will probably all be greater by the time you read this book!

4. John H. Walton, Victor H. Matthews, and Mark W. Chavalas, *IVP Background Commentary: Old Testament* (Downers Grove, IL: IVP Academic, 2000), 527.

5. Gerald H. Wilson, *The NIV Application Commentary: Psalms* Vol. 1 (Grand Rapids, MI: Zondervan, 2002), 670.

6. Ibid., 671.

7. Walton, Matthews, and Chavalas, *IVP Background Commentary*, 527.

8. Ibid., 671.

9. Blaise Pascal, *Good Reads*, accessed June 13, 2021, https://www.goodreads.com/quotes/801132-there-is-a-god -shaped-vacuum-in-the-heart-of-each.

10. *Blue Letter Bible*, accessed June 13, 2021, https:// www.blueletterbible.org/lang/lexicon/lexicon.cfm?Strongs =G5563&t=ESV.

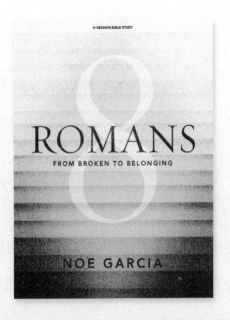

WANT TO SHARE THE MESSAGE OF THIS BOOK WITH OTHERS?

If you know people who are dealing with depression, anxiety, hurting relationships, or unmet expectations, you can help by inviting them to a *Romans 8* Bible study.

Through eight video teaching sessions, Noe Garcia will take your small group on a journey through Romans 8 while sharing his personal experiences of abuse, depression, and overwhelming hopelessness. After each video, your group can use the discussion questions provided in the *Bible Study Books* to further understand the teaching. Guidance for individual prayer and reflection outside the group meeting is also included.

Help others understand Christ's transformative power to repurpose hurt and brokenness for their good and His glory. Learn more online or call 800.458.2772.

Available wherever books are sold